CONTENTS

YELLOWSTONE
WINTER GUIDE

YELLOWSTONE WINTER GUIDE

JEFF HENRY

ROBERTS RINEHART PUBLISHERS
Boulder, Colorado

Text copyright © Jeff Henry 1993, 1998
Photographs copyright © Jeff and Alexa Henry 1993, 1998

Published by ROBERTS RINEHART PUBLISHERS
6309 Monarch Park Place
Niwot, Colorado 80503
TEL 303.652.2685
FAX 303.652.2689
www.robertsrinehart.com

Distributed to the trade by Publishers Group West

Published in Ireland and the UK by
ROBERTS RINEHART PUBLISHERS
Trinity House, Charleston Road
Dublin 6, Ireland

Book design: Ann W. Douden
Maps and charts: Hugh Anderson

International Standard Book Number 1-57098-254-6
Library of Congress Catalog Number 98-86610

10 9 8 7 6 5 4 3 2 1

Printed in Hong Kong

COVER PHOTOGRAPH: UPPER GEYSER BASIN
PAGE I PHOTOGRAPH: COYOTE TRACKS, HAYDEN VALLEY
PAGE III PHOTOGRAPH: COW ELK AND OLD FAITHFUL GEYSER AT
SUNRISE, UPPER GEYSER BASIN

FROSTY COW AND
CALF BISON,
BISCUIT BASIN

THE GREATER YELLOWSTONE
NATIONAL PARK AREA

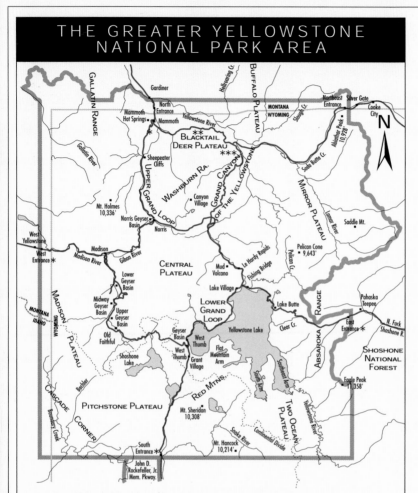

* Open for automobiles from approximately April 15 to November 1. Open for oversnow travel approximately mid-December to mid-March.

** Open in winter for skiers only.

*** Road closed from about Nov. 1 to April 30. Open in winter for skiers only.

Yellowstone in Winter

Yellowstone National Park is situated on a high plateau approximately halfway between the equator and the North Pole. Not surprisingly, winter comes early and stays long in the park; snow usually begins to accumulate on the ground in early November and in most locations lingers until May or June. Temperatures as low as -66°F have been officially recorded, and even lower unofficial readings have been made.

Park roads are maintained for wheeled vehicles until the first heavy snowfall after October 31. That event closes roads for approximately five to six weeks to give Mother Nature time to pile up a base of snow for winter travel. The park opens for over-the-snow traffic in mid-December. Old Faithful Snow Lodge and Yellowstone Park Service Stations gasoline service commence operation at about the same time. Mammoth Hot Springs Hotel opens for business a week or so later, usually just a few days before Christmas.

The noteworthy exception to this road maintenance schedule is the park road between Gardiner, Montana, at Yellowstone's North Gate, and Cooke City, Montana, at the park's Northeast Gate, which is open for wheeled vehicles year-round. This road is approximately 55 miles long and a trip over it in winter offers superb wildlife viewing opportunities. Some people see the Cooke City road as a preferable alternative to the oversnow travel required elsewhere in the park.

Winter season in Yellowstone lasts about three months. Mammoth Hot Springs Hotel usually closes about the first weekend in March and road plowing from Mammoth begins almost immediately thereafter. March is a transitional month, with snowcoaches and snowmobiles giving way to plow crews who generally work from north to south in the south in the park. Old Faithful Snow Lodge closes around the middle of the month and all oversnow traffic is done by sometime around March 20. Interior park roads begin to reopen for wheeled vehicles in April and are fully open by sometime in May. Exact dates vary a bit from year to year and schedules are always subject to disruption by the weather.

A general map of the greater Yellowstone Park area is on page viii.

COW ELK WITH OLD
FAITHFUL GEYSER
IN DISTANCE,
UPPER GEYSER
BASIN

History of Human Activity
in Winter Yellowstone

Human history in the Yellowstone area begins with the native Americans. Contrary to much that has been written and said, there is no legitimate record of early native Americans avoiding the Yellowstone country out of fear of hydrogeothermal activity. However, evidence does indicate that prehistoric peoples avoided the harsh winters in the interior of what is now Yellowstone National Park. It appears that significant numbers of early native Americans summered in the park area and migrated to lower elevations before winter's onset.

The first Anglo man to visit the Yellowstone headwaters area probably was John Colter, a former member of the Lewis and Clark Expedition. Historians believe Colter passed through the park area in the winter of 1807–1808 on one leg of a herculean 600-mile walk from a fur trading post located east of present-day Billings, Montana.

During the three decades following Colter's trek many other trappers and fur traders traveled through the Yellowstone country in pursuit of their business. But as far as is known, none of these rugged mountain men braved a winter in the Yellowstone high country.

The years following the fur trade era brought prospectors to the northern Rockies. They also passed through Yellowstone in summer and, like the earlier mountain men, wintered in lower, less severe climates.

Yellowstone was officially explored by the U.S. government in the early 1870s and was designated a national park in short order, in 1872. Various hotels and inns soon were constructed to serve the summer visitors who began to come to the new park. Caretakers were hired to watch after these structures in the off season, and these hardy "Winter-keepers," as they were called, were some of the first people to winter in Yellowstone.

Winterkeepers even preceded the first official winter exploration of the park, which didn't occur until the winter of 1886–1887. A party of eight men, including the famous photographer Frank J. Haynes, left Mammoth Hot Springs on January 2, 1887, to visit Norris, the Firehole River Valley, and the Grand Canyon of the Yellowstone River. Unfortunately for the party they embarked during one of the harshest winters in recorded history. Their trip, which was made on heavy wooden skis with toboggans in tow, was so arduous that half of the original group returned to Mammoth after making it only as far as Norris. The remaining four traveled on to the Upper Geyser Basin, returned to Norris, then went east to Canyon, and finally traveled over the Washburn Range to Pleasant Valley, where an innkeeper named John Yancey put them up in his hotel until they recovered sufficient strength to negotiate the remaining 20 miles back to Mammoth. With the assistance of his companions, Haynes had managed to make some remarkable photographs, especially of the hydrogeothermal wonders in the Norris and Upper Geyser Basins, but the rigors of the trip were such that the park superintendent of the day was moved to write that the tour "is not to be recommended as a winter diversion."

LAKE LODGE WINTERKEEPER DALE FOWLER AT EDGE OF YELLOWSTONE LAKE, EARLY WINTER SUNRISE

The attitude that Yellowstone was a good place to avoid in winter persisted for decades—self-reliant winterkeepers and occasional rangers enjoyed the peace and beauty of the place mostly in solitude. Shortly after World War II, however, new technology began to appear on the scene in the form of over-the-snow transportation. The first of these vehicles was a snow plane, a contraption greatly resembling an airboat

designed for cruising through swamps and marshes. In the 1950s, organizers began to conduct sporadic trips from West Yellowstone, Montana, to Old Faithful on snow planes, but winter tours to the park were minimal until the late 1960s, when snowmobiles became common.

With the opening of Old Faithful Snow Lodge in the winter of 1971–1972, and with ever increasing support from the National Park Service in the form of road maintenance for over-the-snow travel, winter visitation began a rapid increase, a trend that continues today.

National Park Service records indicate that less than 1,000 people and only six private snow machines visited the park during the winter of 1963–1964. By 1979–1980, visitation had risen to 50,000 people, including 27,641 snowmobiles. Mammoth Hot Springs Hotel opened for winter business in 1982–1983, and that winter visitors numbered 103,877 with 31,145 snowmobiles. In 1993–1994, winter visitation had climbed to 143,523, including 87,682 who came on snowmobiles. Improved regional transportation systems as well as the growing popularity of outdoor and winter recreation have all contributed to increasing winter use of Yellowstone.

Fundamentally, of course, the attractions are the wildlife, the geothermal features, and the frozen beauty of the park itself.

Getting There

Yellowstone is located in the extreme northwestern corner of Wyoming, with narrow strips of the park spilling over into Montana and Idaho. Commercial airlines, including Northwest, Delta, and Continental, offer year-round service to Jackson and Cody, Wyoming, to Idaho Falls, Idaho, and to Billings and Bozeman, Montana. All these cities are just a few hours' driving time from Yellowstone National Park. Hertz, National, Avis, and other car rental agencies have outlets in these communities.

LOWER FALLS AND GRAND CANYON OF THE YELLOWSTONE

In winter, most airline travellers to Yellowstone fly into either Bozeman or Jackson. Karst Stage of Bozeman, Montana, provides daily bus service in winter from Bozeman to both West Yellowstone and Mammoth Hot Springs. Karst Stage is located at 511 North Wallace Avenue, Bozeman, Montana 59715. The telephone number is (406) 586-8567.

Powder River Bus Lines (175 East Pearl Street, Jackson, Wyoming 83001) runs buses from Jackson to Flagg Ranch at the South Entrance of Yellowstone. Powder River's phone number is (307) 733-3164. Again, service is daily during the winter season.

Lodging, snowmobile rentals, and other services are available at all of the four winter entrances to the park. West Yellowstone and Gardiner, Montana, offer the greatest number of motels and other accommodations in close proximity to the park boundary. Pahaska Teepee and other lodges along the North Fork of the Shoshone River offer lodging and other services outside the East Entrance. Flagg Ranch and a few others do the same outside the South Entrance. Many people arriving at Jackson choose to stay in Jackson, however, until the day they have scheduled to go into the park.

If you choose Yellowstone's North Entrance, you may drive a wheeled vehicle from Gardiner to Mammoth Hot Springs and from there on to Cooke City, Montana, where the plowed road ends. It's a total of 55 miles from Gardiner to Cooke City.

If you choose one of Yellowstone's three other winter entrances, you have three options for travelling into the park: You can ski, take a snowcoach, or drive a snowmobile, either your own or a rental machine.

Snowcoaches are peculiar tracked vehicles that look like overgrown snowmobiles and serve as mass transit in winter Yellowstone. Yellowstone National Park Lodges of Amfac Parks and Resorts operates regular coach runs to Old Faithful from the South, West, and North Entrances. Charter snowcoach service from the East Entrance is possible by prior arrangement with Amfac.

Snowmobile rentals are available at all the park gates. You may rent a snow machine and tour the park as part of a guided group or arrange to rent a machine individually and strike off to explore the park on your own. Snowmobiling accessories such as helmets, snowsuits, and heavy mittens are also available, in some cases at extra cost. Remember that all the over-the-snow vehicles in Yellowstone National Park are restricted to groomed roadways.

Old Faithful Snow Lodge, operated by Amfac, is the only accommodation open for winter business in the interior of the park. The season at Snow Lodge runs from mid-December to mid-March. Winter visitors to the park interior who wish to stay overnight essentially must choose between Snow Lodge and camping out. One other choice is Yellowstone Expeditions, which operates a tent camp at Canyon. For more information about Yellowstone Expeditions and the services it offers, see chapter 4.

Of course, not everyone who goes into Yellowstone desires to stay overnight. Day trips that take in a good portion of the park's major attractions are the choice of many visitors. Most guided snowmobile tours include a circuit of the Lower Loop, a route that includes Old Faithful, the Grand Canyon of the Yellowstone River, the Norris Geyser Basis, and Yellowstone Lake. Amfac operates regularly scheduled Lower Loop tours from Old Faithful Snow Lodge. Charter Lower Loop tours can be arranged from other points of origin. If you are on a snow machine and conducting your own tour, you obviously can travel to points that interest you. Lists of companies that rent snowmobiles at or near the entrances to Yellowstone National Park are on pages 20–22.

Lodging

If you want to stay overnight in Yellowstone National Park in the winter, you have three choices. You can lodge with Amfac Parks and Resorts at either Old Faithful Snow Lodge or the Mammoth Hot Springs Hotel; you can stay in Yellowstone Expeditions' tent camp at Canyon; or you can camp out, either at the auto campground at Mammoth or at other locations, with a permit from the National Park Service.

Amfac Parks and Resorts' room prices range from $65 to $125 per night. That price range applies to both Mammoth Hot Springs Hotel and Old Faithful Snow Lodge. Restaurants, ski rentals, and other services are available at both locations. Mammoth Hotel is accessible by automobile, whereas Old Faithful Snow Lodge can be reached only by oversnow travel. Snow Lodge operates from mid-December until mid-March; Mammoth Hotel's season is shorter by a week to ten days at each end of the winter, roughly December 21 to March 4. Contact Amfac Parks and Resorts, at Mammoth Hot Springs, Yellowstone National Park, Wyoming 82190; the telephone number is (307) 344-7901 or, for reservations, (307) 344-7311.

Yellowstone Expeditions, (406) 646-9333 or 1-800-728-9333, offers an alternative to the standard winter tour of Yellowstone. Arden Bailey and Erica Hutchings, proprietors of Yellowstone Expeditions, run snowcoaches from West Yellowstone, or from other departure points by prior arrangement, to a tent camp at Canyon. Bailey has been in the Yellowstone area for many years and has accumulated a wealth of experience. Their camp at Canyon, situated in a secluded lodgepole pine forest, consists of two large communal tents for dining and socializing and a number of smaller sleeping tents designed for double occupancy. The large tents are heated with woodstoves, the sleeping tents with propane. All the tents are sturdy woodframe structures, and in Yellowstone Expeditions' many years of operation no one has ever complained about being cold while staying at the camp. Guests at the camp enjoy excellent food, snowcoach excursions, and superb cross country skiing in the Canyon area. Yellowstone Expeditions' prices vary according to group size and length of stay. The people of Yellowstone Expeditions and the services they provide are highly recommended.

The campground at Mammoth is the only roadside campground in Yellowstone National Park that is open in winter. Usually there is little competition for the available sites. The National Park Service maintains heated bathrooms (without showers) at the campground.

Individual camping, either at Old Faithful or in the backcountry, is by permit only. Permits have to be procured from a National Park Service ranger station in the park. Good winter camping skills and adequate gear are obvious musts, especially if you plan to camp in the backcountry. Current weather conditions and other important information can be obtained from the Visitor Services Office, U.S. National Park Service, Yellowstone National Park, Wyoming 82190, or by calling (307) 344-7381, extension 2206.

Lodging is also available in all of Yellowstone National Park's gateway communities. Because of transportation schedules and for other reasons, most winter visitors to Yellowstone spend at least one or two nights outside the park. Naturally, prices for lodging outside the park run the gamut. Following is a list of Yellowstone area lodgings including addresses and phone numbers. The list is organized by community.

JACKSON, WYOMING

ALPINE MOTEL
70 South Jean
Jackson, WY 83001
307-733-2082

ANTLER MOTEL
West Pearl and Cache
P. O. Box 575
Jackson, WY 83001
307-733-2535

ANVIL MOTEL
215 North Cache
Jackson, WY 83001
307-733-3668/1-800-234-4507

BEST WESTERN ALPENHOF
Teton Village
Jackson, WY 83001
307-733-3242

BEST WESTERN PARKWAY MOTEL
125 North Jackson
Jackson, WY 83001
307-733-3143

BIG MOUNTAIN INN
3755 North Moose-Wilson Road
Jackson, WY 83001
307-733-1981

BUCKRAIL LODGE
110 East Karns Avenue
Jackson, WY 83001
307-733-2079

GOLDEN EAGLE MOTOR INN
325 East Broadway
Jackson, WY 83001
307-733-2042

CACHE CREEK MOTEL
P.O. Box 918
Jackson, WY 83001
307-733-7781/1-800-843-4788

HITCHING POST LODGE
460 East Broadway
Jackson, WY 83001
307-733-2606

COWBOY VILLAGE RESORT
120 South Flat Creek Drive
Jackson, WY 83001
307-733-3121

THE INN AT JACKSON HOLE
Teton Village
Jackson, WY 83001
307-733-2311

ELK COUNTRY INN
480 West Pearl
Jackson, WY 83001
307-733-0336

JACKSON HOLE LODGE
420 West Broadway
Jackson, WY 83001
307-733-2992/1-800-642-4567

ELK REFUGE INN
Highway 89
Jackson, WY 83001
307-733-3582

OUTLAW MOTEL
265 South Millward
Jackson, WY 83001
307-733-3682

FLAGG RANCH
Moran, WY 83013
307-733-8761/733-1572
307-543-2861/1-800-443-231

PAINTED BUFFALO
400 West Broadway
Jackson, WY 83001
307-733-4340

FLAT CREEK MOTEL
1935 North Highway 89
Jackson, WY 83001
307-733-5276

PARKWAY MOTEL
125 North Jackson
Jackson, WY 83001
307-733-3143

49ER INN
West Pearl and Jackson
P.O. Box 1948
Jackson, WY 83001
307-733-7550

PONY EXPRESS MOTEL
50 South Millward
P.O. Box 972
Jackson, WY 83001

PROSPECTOR MOTEL
155 North Jackson
Jackson, WY 83001
307-733-4858

FOUR WINDS MOTEL
150 North Millward
Jackson, WY 83001
307-733-2474

CROSS COUNTRY
SKIERS PREPARE
FOR SKI TRIP
WHILE TOURING
PARK WITH
YELLOWSTONE
EXPEDITIONS

RANCH INN
45 East Pearl Street
Jackson, WY 83001
307-733-6363

RAWHIDE MOTEL
75 South Millward
Jackson, WY 83001
307-733-1216

SAGEBRUSH MOTEL
550 West Broadway
Jackson, WY 83001
307-733-0336

SNOW KING LODGE MOTEL
470 King
Jackson, WY 83001
307-733-3480

SNOW KING RESORT HOTEL
400 East Snow King Avenue
Jackson, WY 83001
307-733-5200

SOJOURNER INN
Teton Village
Jackson, WY 83001
307-733-3657

SUNDANCE INN
135 West Broadway
Jackson, WY 83001
307-733-3444

TETON GABLES MOTEL
1140 West Highway 22
Jackson, WY 83001
307-733-3723

TETON TREEHOUSE
BED & BREAKFAST
Wilson, WY 83014
307-733-3233

TETON VIEW BED & BREAKFAST
2136 Coyote Loop
Jackson, WY 83001
307-733-7954

TRAPPER INN
235 North Cache Drive
Jackson, WY 83001
307-733-2648

THE VIRGINIAN LODGE
750 West Broadway
Jackson, WY 83001
307-733-2792/733-7189
1-800-262-4999

WAGON WHEEL VILLAGE MOTEL
435 North Cache
Jackson, WY 83001
307-733-2357

WESTERN MOTEL
225 South Glenwood
Jackson, WY 83001
307-733-3291

WOOD'S MOTEL
120 North Glenwood
Jackson, WY 83001
307-733-2953

THE WORT HOTEL
Broadway and Glenwood
Jackson, WY 83001
307-733-2190

**WEST YELLOWSTONE,
MONTANA**

AMBASSADOR QUALITY INN
315 Yellowstone Avenue
West Yellowstone, MT 59758
406-646-7365

BEST WESTERN EXECUTIVE INN
236 Dunraven
West Yellowstone, MT 59758
406-646-7681

BEST WESTERN WESTON INN
103 Gibbon Avenue
West Yellowstone, MT 59758
406-646-7373
1-800-528-1234

BIG WESTERN PINE
234 Firehole Avenue
West Yellowstone, MT 59758
406-646-7622

BRANDIN' IRON MOTEL
201 Canyon
West Yellowstone, MT 59758
406-646-9411
1-800-231-5991

BUCKBOARD MOTEL
119 Electric
West Yellowstone, MT 59758
406-646-9020

CROSS WINDS INN
201 Firehole Avenue
West Yellowstone, MT 59758
406-646-9557

DAYS INN
118 Electric Street
West Yellowstone, MT 59758
406-646-7656
1-800-548-9551

DESERT INN MOTEL
133 Canyon
West Yellowstone, MT 59758
406-646-7376

DUDE MOTOR INN
3 Madison Avenue
West Yellowstone, MT 59758
406-646-7201

GOLDEN WEST MOTEL
429 Madison Avenue
West Yellowstone, MT 59758
406-646-7778

GRAY WOLF INN AND SUITES
250 South Canyon
West Yellowstone, MT 59758
406-646-7656
1-800-852-8602

HO HUM MOTEL
126 Canyon
West Yellowstone, MT 59758
406-646-7746

KELLY INN
104 South Canyon Street
West Yellowstone, MT 59758
406-646-7746
1-800-259-4672

LIONSHEAD RESORT
1545 Targhee Pass Highway
West Yellowstone, MT 59758
406-646-7296

PINE SHADOWS MOTEL
530 Gibbon Avenue
West Yellowstone, MT 59758
406-646-7541

PONY EXPRESS MOTEL
4 Firehole Avenue
West Yellowstone, MT 59758
406-646-7644
1-800-323-9708

ROUNDUP MOTEL
3 Madison Avenue
West Yellowstone, MT 59758
406-646-7301
1-800-833-SNOW

SLEEPY HOLLOW LODGE
124 Electric
West Yellowstone, MT 59758
406-646-7707

STAGE COACH INN
209 Madison Avenue
West Yellowstone, MT 59758
406-646-7381/1-800-842-2882

THREE BEAR LODGE
217 Yellowstone Avenue
West Yellowstone, MT 59758
406-646-7353

TRAVELER'S LODGE
225 Yellowstone Avenue
West Yellowstone, MT 59758
406-646-9561
1-800-831-5741

WESTWOOD MOTEL
238 Madison Avenue
P.O. Box L
West Yellowstone, MT 59758
406-646-7713

THE WHISPERING PINES MOTEL
321 Canyon
West Yellowstone, MT 59758
406-646-9317

THE MAMMOTH HOT SPRINGS AND GARDINER, MONTANA, AREA

BEST WESTERN
Highway 89
Gardiner, MT 59030
406-848-7311/848-7557

BLUE HAVEN MOTEL
Gardiner, MT 59030
406-848-7719

SUPER 8 MOTEL
Highway 89
Gardiner, MT 59030
406-848-7401

WESTERNAIRE MOTEL
Gardiner, MT 59030
406-848-7397
406-848-7397

YELLOWSTONE NATIONAL PARK
LODGES, AMFAC PARKS AND
RESORTS
Mammoth Hot Springs,
Yellowstone N.P., WY 81290
307-344-7901/344-7311

YELLOWSTONE VILLAGE INN
Gardiner, MT 59030
406-848-7417

**THE SILVER GATE AND
COOKE CITY, MONTANA,
AREA**

ALPINE MOTEL
Cooke City, MT 59020
406-838-2262

BEARCLAW CABINS
Cooke City, MT 59020
406-838-2336

ELK HORN MOTEL & CABINS
Cooke City, MT 59020
406-838-2332

GRIZZLY LODGE
Silver Gate, MT 59081
406-838-2219

HIGH COUNTRY MOTEL
Cooke City, MT 59020
406-838-2272

HOOSIER'S MOTEL
Cooke City, MT 59020
406-838-2241

PARKVIEW MOTEL
Silver Gate, MT 59081
406-838-2371

SODA BUTTE LODGE
Cooke City, MT 59020
406-838-2251

NORTH FORK OF THE SHOSHONE RIVER (INCLUDING CODY, WYOMING)

Along the North Fork

ABSAROKA MOUNTAIN LODGE
1231 Yellowstone Highway
Wapiti, WY 82450
307-587-3963

BILL CODY'S RANCH RESORT
2604CC Yellowstone Highway
Cody, WY 82414
307-587-2097

BLACKWATER LODGE
1516 Northfork Highway
Cody, WY 82414
307-587-5201

CASTLE ROCK CENTRE RANCH
412 Road 6NS
Cody, WY 82414
307-587-2076
1-800-356-9965

MOUNTAIN VIEW LODGE
Northfork Route
Wapiti, WY 82450
307-587-2081

PAHASKA TEEPEE RESORT
183 Yellowstone Highway
Cody, WY 82414
307-527-7701

SHOSHONE LODGE
Box 790, Yellowstone Highway
Cody, WY 82414
307-587-4044

IN CODY

BEST WESTERN SUNSET
1601 8th Street
Cody, WY 82414
307-587-4265

BIG BEAR MOTEL
P. O. Box 2015
Cody, WY 82414
307-587-3117

CAROLINE LOCKHART'S BED
& BREAKFAST INN
109 West Yellowstone Avenue
Cody, WY 82414
307-587-6074

HOLIDAY INN
1701 Sheridan Avenue
Cody, WY 82414
307-587-5555

HOLIDAY MOTEL
1807 Sheridan Avenue
Cody, WY 82414
307-587-4258

IRMA HOTEL
1192 Sheridan Avenue
Cody, WY 82414
307-587-4221

PAWNEE LODGE
1032 12th Street
Cody, WY 82414
307-587-2239

UPTOWN MOTEL
1562 Sheridan Avenue
Cody, WY 82414
307-587-4245

Snowmobiling

More than half the people who come to Yellowstone in winter tour the park on snowmobiles. Most rent snowmobiles from Amfac Parks and Resorts at the Mammoth Hot Springs Hotel or from one of the many businesses renting machines in the park's gateway communities (a list of snowmobile rental businesses is on pages 20–22). It is permissible to bring your own snow machine to Yellowstone. Private machines must be licensed in their state of origin, and the National Park Service charges an entry fee of $10 per person ($15 per snow machine with two people) for touring on the park's groomed roads. The fee is good for a seven-day period, so save your receipt if you plan to return to the park within that length of time.

It should be pointed out that snowmobiling in Yellowstone is considered a means of access to the park's wonders and should not be considered an end in itself. Snowmobiling as a sport in and of itself is best pursued elsewhere. Island Park, Idaho, and some areas west of West Yellowstone, Montana, such as Two Top Mountain are examples of areas that have been devoted to off-trail snowmobiling; snowmobiling enthusiasts may wish to allot some of their time in the Yellowstone country to recreating in those areas. In Yellowstone National Park, snowmobiles are restricted to groomed roadways and to a 45-mile-per-hour speed limit. National Park Service rangers enforce all regulations pertaining to snowmobiling.

Rental snowmobiles cost in the neighborhood of $75–$140 per day. Rates vary according to whether machines are rented with or without a guide, what accessories (e.g., snowmobile suits) are requested with the machines, whether machines will be ridden individually or whether people plan to "double up," and other factors. Most rental outlets offer half-day rates, too. Rental costs in Jackson tend to be higher than those in West Yellowstone, because outfitters in Jackson have to haul their machines to and from Flagg Ranch (about 110 miles round-trip) on a daily basis. Most of these outfitters offer transportation to and from Flagg Ranch for clients, too. Snowmobilers from West Yellowstone are able to drive their machines directly from rental lots to the park gate over that town's snowpacked roads.

Reputable snowmobile rental businesses usually run machines that are no more than two or three years old. That's nice to know because a snowmobile trip into Yellowstone Park can take a rider to places 40 miles or so from the nearest plowed road. However, the risk of a breakdown with a snowmobile is always present. Especially if you bring your own machine to the park, it is strongly recommended that you carry some basic repair tools and replacement parts with you. A spare drive belt, a replacement headlight, spark plugs, and the tools to effect such repairs would be a bare minimum. A flashlight or a head-lamp with dependable batteries is a necessity, too.

SNOWMOBILE
PARKING LOT,
OLD FAITHFUL
VISITOR CENTER

CHART OF WINDCHILL TEMPERATURES

ACTUAL THERMOMETER READING IN DEGREES FAHRENHEIT												
50	**40**	**30**	**20**	**10**	**0**	**-10**	**-20**	**-30**	**-40**	**-50**	**-60**	
EQUIVALENT TEMPERATURE, °F												
calm	50	40	30	20	10	0	-10	-20	-30	-40	-50	-60
5	48	37	27	16	6	-5	-15	-26	-36	-47	-57	-68
10	40	28	16	4	-5	-21	-33	-46	-58	-70	-83	-95
15	36	22	9	-5	-18	-36	-45	-58	-72	-85	-99	-112
20	32	18	4	-10	-25	-39	-53	-67	-82	-96	-110	-124
25	30	16	0	-15	-29	-44	-59	-74	-88	-104	-118	-133
30	28	13	-2	-18	-33	-48	-63	-79	-94	-109	-125	-140
35	27	11	-4	-20	-35	-49	-67	-82	-98	-113	-129	-145
40	26	10	-6	-21	-37	-53	-69	-85	-100	-116	-132	-148

WINDSPEED IN MPH

WIND SPEEDS GREATER THAN 40 MPH HAVE LITTLE ADDITIONAL EFFECT

LITTLE DANGER (FOR A PROPERLY CLOTHED PERSON)

INCREASING DANGER

GREAT DANGER

DANGER FROM FREEZING OF EXPOSED FLESH

Temperatures in Yellowstone can be severely cold—most winters see at least a few days of -30°F to -40°F. Air temperatures that low, coupled with the wind speeds engendered by riding a snowmobile up to 45 miles per hour, can produce lethal chill factors (see the windchill chart above). Your comfort, if not your safety, depends on proper clothing and gear. If you are inexperienced with snowmobiling, ask some questions about what constitutes adequate clothing. A typical day tour in Yellowstone amounts to well over 100 miles of snowmobiling, which can be an awfully long and cold trip if you're improperly prepared.

It pays to watch your fuel gauge while snowmobiling in the park, too. Gasoline is available at all the park gates as well as at Old Faithful, Canyon, and Mammoth Hot Springs. If you watch your gauge and fuel as necessary, you shouldn't have any problems. Gasoline is now available at Fishing Bridge, too. If, however, you pass one of the interior gas stations without refueling, you may run out of gas before you get to the next way station.

The Yellowstone Park Service Stations at Old Faithful, Canyon, and Mammoth Hot Springs also stock snowmobile oil and some basic replacement parts. Prices are comparable to what you would pay in other snowmobiling resort areas. Hours of operation at these stations are roughly mid-morning until late afternoon.

At Madison, West Thumb, Fishing Bridge, and Canyon you will find warming huts operated by the National Park Service (NPS). These are good places to stop to stretch, warm up, get a light snack, ask directions, or question an NPS employee about the park. The warming huts at Madison and Canyon offer snack food—some microwaveable by an attendant—and the huts at Fishing Bridge and West Thumb offer vending machine refreshments. Ranger-naturalists are usually on duty at all four warming huts, from 9:00 a.m. until 3:00 p.m.

As you travel around the park, it is quite likely you will encounter wildlife—coyotes, elk, and especially bison—on the groomed roadways. Animals like to walk the hardpacked road surface a lot more than they like to wallow through three to five feet of unpacked snow. Wildlife on the road have the right-of-way, and you must wait for them to move off in their own time. Waiting for wildlife to move out of the way may be inconvenient, but remember that the park is their home and that they are probably a primary reason you came to Yellowstone in the first place. Subtle energy savings and losses in winter are literally matters of life and death for these animals, so give them every consideration.

The following lists provide snowmobile rental businesses that operate in the Yellowstone Park area. The list is organized by community.

RENTALS IN WEST YEL- LOWSTONE, MONTANA (ZIP CODE 59758)

HI COUNTRY SNOWMOBILE
RENTAL
Highway 20 and Hayden
406-646-2541/1-800-624-5291

RENDEZVOUS SNOWMOBILE
RENTALS
429 Yellowstone Avenue
406-646-9564/1-800-426-7669

STAGE COACH INN
209 Madison Avenue
406-646-7381

THREE BEAR LODGE
& RESTAURANT
217 Yellowstone Avenue
406-646-7353/1-800-221-1151

TRAVELER'S LODGE
225 Yellowstone Avenue
406-646-9561/1-800-831-5741

TWO-TOP RENTALS
645 Gibbon Avenue
406-646-7802

WEST YELLOWSTONE
CONFERENCE HOTEL
315 Yellowstone Avenue
406-646-7365

WESTGATE AUTO SNOWMOBILE
RENTAL
11 Yellowstone Avenue
406-646-7651

YELLOWSTONE ADVENTURES
131 Dunraven
406-646-7735/1-800-231-5991

YELLOWSTONE ARCTIC
CAT–YAMAHA
208 Electric Street
406-646-9636

YELLOWSTONE SNOWMOBILES
3 Madison Avenue
406-646-7301

**RENTALS IN JACKSON,
WYOMING (ZIP CODE
83001)**

BEST ADVENTURES
SNOWMOBILE TOURS
P.O. Box 835
Jackson, WY
307-733-4845/1-800-851-0827

CACHE CREEK SNOWMOBILE
1075 South Highway 89
Jackson, WY
307-733-4743

GROTTO GEYSER,
UPPER GEYSER
BASIN

EAGLE SNOWMOBILE RENTALS
375 North Cache Drive
Jackson, WY
307-739-9999/1-800-582-2128

FLAGG RANCH VILLAGE
South Entrance of Yellowstone
Moran, WY 83013
307-543-2861/1-800-443-2311

FORT JACKSON SNOWMOBILE
TOURS
Jackson, WY
307-733-2583/1-800-735-8430

HEART 6
P.O. Box 70, Buffalo Valley Road
Moran, WY
307-543-2477

HIGH COUNTRY SNOWMOBILE
TOURS
P.O. Box 7453
307-733-5017/1-800-524-0130

LEISURE SPORTS
1075 South Highway 89
Jackson, WY
307-733-5351

MOUNTAIN HIGH ADVENTURES
P.O. Box 4084
Jackson, WY
307-733-5351

OLD FAITHFUL SNOWMOBILE
TOURS
750 West Broadway
Jackson, WY
307-733-9767

ROCKY MOUNTAIN SNOWMOBILE
TOURS
1050 South Highway 89
Jackson, WY
307-733-2237/1-800-647-2561

TOGWOTEE SNOWMOBILE
TOURS
P.O. Box 91
Moran, WY 83013
307-733-8800/1-800-543-2847

**RENTALS IN MAMMOTH
HOT SPRINGS AND
GARDINER, MONTANA**

AMFAC PARKS AND RESORTS
Mammoth Hot Springs
Yellowstone N.P., WY 82190
307-344-7901

BEST WESTERN MOTEL
Gardiner, MT 59030
406-848-7557

**RENTALS IN COOKE
CITY, MONTANA**

EXXON GAS STATION/RICKY
SUMMERS
Cooke City, MT 59020
406-838-2244

RENTALS IN THE EAST ENTRANCE AREA

ABSAROKA MOUNTAIN LODGE
1231 Yellowstone Highway
Wapiti, WY 82450
307-587-3963

BILL CODY'S RANCH RESORT
2604CC Yellowstone Highway
Cody, WY 82414
307-587-2097

BLACKWATER LODGE
1516 Northfork Highway
Cody, WY 82414
307-587-5201

CASTLE ROCK CENTRE RANCH
412 Road 6NS
Cody, WY 82414
307-587-2076/1-800-356-9965

MOUNTAIN VIEW LODGE
Northfork Route
Wapiti, WY 82450
307-587-2081

PAHASKA TEEPEE RESORT
183 Yellowstone Highway
Cody, WY 82414
307-527-7701

SHOSHONE LODGE
Box 790, Yellowstone Highway
Cody, WY 82414
307-587-4044

SIX

Mile by Mile
Yellowstone's Roads in Winter

FRIGID (-50°F)
WINTER SUNRISE
AT YELLOWSTONE
LAKE

The following sections offer descriptions of what you might hope to see along various segments of the road system in Yellowstone. Some historical anecdotes are included as well. The descriptions and anecdotes are by no means comprehensive. The account begins at the West Entrance of the park and works inward to Grand Loop Road. The map on page viii shows these road segments within the whole of Yellowstone National Park.

WEST YELLOW-STONE TO MADISON JUNCTION (14 MILES OVERSNOW)

At the edge of the town of West Yellowstone is the West Entrance Station. Here you will be greeted by a representative of the National Park Service, who will charge you a $10 entrance fee (unless you have a

Golden Eagle, Golden Age, or Golden Access Passport) and give you a
sheaf of information about the park.

Two to 3 miles east of the entrance you will begin to see blackened
dead trees. They mark the passage of the great North Fork Fire, which
burned through this area in August and September 1988 and which for
a time threatened the town of West Yellowstone itself. The North Fork
was one of several fires that summer that started outside Yellowstone
and then burned into the park. By November 1988 the fire had grown
to nearly 400,000 acres from its beginning as a carelessly discarded
cigarette in Idaho's Targhee National Forest.

Soon you will see the Madison River on your left. The Madison, like
a number of other rivers in Yellowstone, never freezes no matter how
cold the weather gets. As with many of the other rivers, this is because
so much of the Madison's flow comes from geothermal sources.

Seven miles from West Yellowstone you will cross the Madison on
what is appropriately called Seven Mile Bridge. This is a good place to
look for trumpeter swans and other waterfowl. To the south, on the
other side of the river, you can see the
escarpment that marks the northern edge of
the Madison Plateau. If you haven't seen elk
and bison already, you probably will soon.
The Madison Valley is important winter
range for these animals.

Fourteen miles from West Yellowstone
you'll arrive at Madison Junction. A short
distance south of the road junction is an
important river junction where the Firehole
River arrives from the south and meets the
Gibbon River from the north, forming the
Madison River. Rising prominently above the
river junction is National Park Mountain.
Members of a government exploration party
camped in this vicinity on September 19,
1870, and some legends have it that the idea
for designating the surrounding area a
national park sprang from their campfire
conversations.

The warming hut at Madison offers
snacks and a place to stretch and warm up.
Employees on duty can answer any questions that may have occurred to you up to
this point.

MADISON JUNCTION TO OLD FAITHFUL
(16 MILES OVERSNOW)

A short distance south of Madison Junction is a side road through Firehole Canyon. This canyon marks the spot where the Firehole River runs down off the Madison Plateau. A mile or so south of the exit from Firehole Canyon Drive you will see Christmas Tree Rock in the river. As the name implies, this feature looks like a Christmas tree on a rock. This stretch of road is a likely place to meet or overtake bison moving between the Madison Junction area and other winter ranges higher up the Firehole Valley.

Either choice will soon bring you in sight of the first of the great geyser basins. If the day is clear and cold, the towering columns of steam from Lower Geyser Basin will be impressive. Equally impressive will be the wildlife in and around the Fountain Flats area. In winter, the groups of bison you see on and around Fountain Flats are apt to be the largest you will find anywhere in the park.

CHRISTMAS TREE ROCK IN THE FIREHOLE RIVER IS ONE OF YELLOWSTONE'S SMALL WONDERS

Just south of Fountain Flats, a stop at Fountain Paint Pots is a good choice. A short walk around the boardwalk here will introduce you to the four general types of hydrothermal features: geysers, hot springs, mudpots, and fumaroles (steam vents). Interpretive pamphlets for the Paint Pots area are available for 25¢ where the boardwalk leaves the parking lot.

A mile south of Fountain Paint Pots, Grand Loop Road crosses White Creek. A number of lodgepole pines have been killed by shifting geothermal runoff channels along this stream. Some people call these "bobby sox" trees; a look at the trees will tell you why. The White Creek area is an excellent place to spot large bull elk in winter.

Beyond White Creek the road crosses Whiskey Flats, where stagecoach drivers reputedly stashed the whiskey that company policy prohibited. This is another likely place to find wildlife on the road. You may notice on your tour that elk and bison are most likely to be found travelling the road between thermal basins. The animals forage on geothermally bared ground in the basins and use connecting roads as travel corridors.

Midway Geyser Basin, so named because it is midway between the Upper and Lower Geyser Basins, will soon appear on your right. Another boardwalk bridges the Firehole River here and leads through the hiss and gurgle of the various springs. Most noteworthy are Grand Prismatic Spring, named for its variegated colors, and Excelsior Spring. The latter was at one time a prodigious geyser, but because of human abuse long ago, it degenerated to a flowing hot spring. But Excelsior Spring is still a remarkable feature—it discharges over 4,000 gallons of hot water per minute. You can see the algae-colored runoff channels from Excelsior on the other side of the river just upstream from the footbridge.

About a mile south of the Midway Geyser Basin parking area, the Grand Loop Road crosses Rabbit Creek, a stream whose waters come almost exclusively from geothermal runoff. This area marks the mouth of Rabbit Creek, a stream whose waters came almost exclusively from geothermal runoff. This area is favored by grizzly bears when they emerge from hibernation in late March and April. Rabbit Creek flows into the Firehole from the east.

A half mile south of the crossing of Rabbit Creek, the road enters a lodgepole pine forest. Almost always, there are bison and cow elk present in the first half mile of this forest, most often on the right side of the road. The wooded area extends for the next 3 miles or so. Several small, mostly tepid springs are along this stretch of road and these seem to be attractive to large bull bison, for they are usually seen thereabouts.

The forest opens up at Biscuit Basin, another likely place to see adult bull elk. From Biscuit Basin the road continues on past Black Sand Basin and finally reaches the turnoff to the Old Faithful developed area and, of course, the famous geyser itself. At Old Faithful is the Snow Lodge, offering food, lodging, and a gift shop; a Yellowstone Park Service Station with fuel; and a National Park Service Visitor Center and Ranger Station. The visitor center offers interpretive programs and information as well as books for sale. Backcountry use permits for overnight camping trips, information, and emergency assistance can be obtained at the ranger station.

OLD FAITHFUL TO WEST THUMB
(17 MILES OVERSNOW)

About a mile toward West Thumb, Grand Loop Road passes Kepler Cascades on the Firehole River. The cascades were named for a young boy who visited the park in the late nineteenth century. In the vicinity are some fire-killed trees, victims of the North Fork Fire that stormed through here on September 7, 1988.

The road rises in elevation through coniferous forests mostly devoid of wildlife until you arrive at Isa Lake, a small pond that sits astride the Continental Divide and that has the distinction of draining to both the Atlantic and the Pacific Oceans. You will be 8,261 feet high at Isa Lake.

Almost exactly halfway between Old Faithful and West Thumb is Shoshone Point, named for the large backcountry lake visible to the south. On a clear day you'll be able to see the Teton Range in the distance beyond the lake.

BULL BISON ALONG
THE FIREHOLE
RIVER AT SUNSET,
BISCUIT BASIN

A few miles beyond Shoshone Point you will cross the Continental Divide again. You will be back in the drainage of the Atlantic Ocean after you do, and it will be only another 4 miles or so until you'll have your first view of Yellowstone Lake and the Absaroka Mountains east of the lake. Yellowstone is a huge lake for its elevation of 7,733 feet. It's remarkable there is enough land that is higher still to catch sufficient rain and snow to fill the lake's basin.

West Thumb Junction is next. Continuing south from here will take you to South Entrance and Flagg Ranch (2 miles of snow-packed road beyond South Entrance); turning left will keep you on the Grand Loop Road. The West Thumb warming hut is situated just east of the junction and adjacent to the West Thumb Geyser Basin. Vending machines and a park interpreter are available at the hut.

WEST THUMB TO FISHING BRIDGE
(21 MILES OVERSNOW)

Thermal activity around West Thumb and the Potts Thermal Area just to the east keeps breather holes open in the Yellowstone Lake ice. Otters congregate in the area to fish for Yellowstone Lake cutthroat trout through the open water. Coyotes, ravens, and bald eagles also gather here either to steal fish from the otters or to scavenge scraps the otters leave behind. The actions and interactions of these animals make for a grand show, if

SNOWCOACH DRIVER JOHN SALVATO WITH GUESTS AT WEST THUMB

you're lucky enough to catch it. Early and late in the day are the best times to see the otters and their associates.

Beyond the Potts Thermal Area, where you might see signs of a wintering moose or two, the road enters a coniferous forest that continues for most of the 21 miles between West Thumb and Fishing Bridge. The road parallels the lakeshore all the way, and breaks in the timber offer frequent vistas of the lake and distant mountains. The range due south of the lake and the mountains closest to you when you leave West Thumb are the Red Mountains, the principal peak of which is Mount Sheridan. Farther east, views of the rugged Absarokas to the east of the lake will become more frequent. The Absarokas trend north and south and in this sector approximate the eastern boundary of Yellowstone National Park.

Two miles past Bridge Bay, you will pass the turnoff to Lake Village, all of which is closed in winter. Another 1.5 miles and you will be at Fishing Bridge Junction, where you can either turn right and travel 26 miles to East Entrance (and 2 more miles of snowpacked road beyond that to the Pahaska Teepee Resort or continue north on Grand Loop Road. The Fishing Bridge warming hut is about 1 mile down the road toward East Entrance and offers pretty much the same services as the one at West Thumb. A Yellowstone Park Service Station is situated across the road and 100 yards west of the warming hut.

FISHING BRIDGE TO CANYON
(16 MILES OVERSNOW)

The first 2 miles of road north of Fishing Bridge pass through a mature lodgepole pine forest. Where the forest breaks open into a meadow the Yellowstone River will be immediately on your right. Depending on the month and on recent weather patterns, this stretch of river may be either open or frozen. If open, it's a good place to see waterfowl, including trumpeter swans, Canada geese, and a variety of ducks. A good pair of binoculars and a field guide to birds are assets at this point. Below the open meadow the Yellowstone cascades over Le Hardy Rapids. An explorer by that name wrecked his raft and lost his shotgun in these rapids in the summer of 1873.

Three miles below Le Hardy Rapids is Buffalo Ford, well named for the shaggy beasts that are frequently seen here at all seasons of the year. You almost certainly will see some of them in the meadow between Buffalo Ford and Mud Volcano. The latter is the name of a particular feature and the surrounding thermal area. For wildlife the area is an oasis of snow-free ground on the edge of the frozen expanse of Hayden Valley to the north.

The next 4 or 5 miles of road lead through Hayden Valley, in some respects the harshest landscape you will see on your trip through Yellowstone. Mostly treeless and completely snow covered, the valley is subject to frequent strong winds and blowing snow. The road through the valley is sometimes closed in winter because of storms and lack of visibility. Other than bird life along the river, the only wildlife you are likely to see are bison and possibly a coyote or two. It is a testament to the hardiness of the former and the resourcefulness of the latter that they are able to survive in this beautifully austere place.

Alum Creek marks the northern end of Hayden Valley. The mouth of the creek is an excellent place to spot waterfowl, as is the stretch of the Yellowstone River from Alum Creek down to the Chittenden Bridge. This stretch of river offers one of your best chances for seeing trumpeter swans and it's one of the best areas for spotting bald eagles. Otters are sometimes seen here, too.

Two miles south of Canyon Junction is the turnoff to the Chittenden Bridge and the South Rim of the Grand Canyon of the Yellowstone River. Spectacular views of the canyon and of the Upper and Lower Falls are found along the South Rim Drive, a 2-mile road that dead-ends. You have to retrace this road to return to Grand Loop Road.

Canyon Junction has a warming hut and a Yellowstone Park Service Station. Fueling here before you continue in any direction is a good idea as it's a minimum of 33 miles to the next fuel (at Mammoth Hot Springs). The warming hut at Canyon is staffed by an attendant who

dispenses coffee, sandwiches, microwaved popcorn, and the like. A
National Park Service employee is usually nearby, too.

RED FOX TRACKS
IN SNOW, HAYDEN
VALLEY

North Rim Drive around the canyon begins at the warming hut and
leads one way to vistas that complement the ones you had from the
South Rim. This road will take you back to Grand Loop Road 1.5 miles
south of Canyon, from which point you'll need to travel north to return
to Canyon Junction.

North of Canyon Junction the road toward Dunraven Pass is open
only for the first 2 miles to the Washburn Hot Springs Overlook. From
here you can see Washburn Hot Springs below and gain another look
at the Absaroka Mountain Range to the east, after which you'll have to
make a U-turn and go back to Canyon.

CANYON TO NORRIS (12 MILES OVERSNOW)

Norris is 12 miles west of Canyon at the end of a highway that
leads through mostly lodgepole pine forest. Except at the very beginning and very end of the 12 miles, you probably won't see much
wildlife. The stretch of country between Canyon and Norris is relatively
high in elevation and little influenced by geothermal activity. Therefore,
it is largely inhospitable for wintering wildlife. The large numbers of
dead trees along this road were killed by the Wolf Lake Fire, an off-
shoot of the North Fork Fire, in August and September 1988.

At Norris you will find the Norris Geyser Basin, the hottest and most active geyser basin in the world and the home of Steamboat Geyser, the world's tallest. A series of boardwalks lead through the basin and interpretive pamphlets (25¢) are available at the start of your walk.

NORRIS TO MADISON JUNCTION
(14 MILES OVERSNOW)

South of Norris, Grand Loop Road passes through more burned trees before entering Elk Park. Not surprisingly, you have a good chance of seeing elk in this vicinity. Any elk you see will almost certainly be cows and young, for adult bulls do not frequent this area in winter. The stream in Elk Park is the Gibbon River, named for Colonel John Gibbon, a U.S. Army officer who first passed this way in 1871.

The next large meadow on the road to Madison is Gibbon Meadow. The steaming thermals on the far side of the meadow are Sylvan Springs. Elk are almost always in sight somewhere in Gibbon Meadow. You may see a few bull bison as well. The south end of the meadow, where the river enters Gibbon Canyon, is a good place to spot bald eagles.

Gibbon Canyon extends from Gibbon Meadow south toward Madison Junction. The canyon is winter home to a number of mature bull elk. These bulls often offer great photo opportunities, but please don't approach them closely or otherwise disturb them.

You will soon see Gibbon Falls on your left. It marks the spot where the Gibbon River drops off higher plateau country on its way down to Madison Junction, which is 4 miles south of the falls.

FISHING BRIDGE TO EAST ENTRANCE/PAHASKA
TEEPEE (28 MILES OVERSNOW)

A couple of miles east of Fishing Bridge Junction, East Entrance Road crosses Pelican Creek. You are likely to see bison here, probably large bulls and possibly some females and young as well. Until a few years ago this area was winter range for bulls exclusively, but in recent winters cows and young have begun to appear here, too. The island you can see in Yellowstone Lake from the Pelican Creek bridge is Stevenson Island, named for an explorer who launched a prefabricated boat on the lake in 1871. From the bridge or from the turnouts at either side of the Pelican Estuary it is sometimes possible to make dramatic photographs with bison in the foreground and the frozen lake and mountains in the background.

Beyond Pelican Creek the road passes through a couple of more miles of lodgepole pine forest before breaking out into the Indian Pond Meadows. You'll see more bison in the meadows and especially around

Indian Pond itself. Indian Pond fills what geologists call a steam explosion crater, which is a spot where pent-up geothermal pressure has been released in a violent extrusive event. The pond and its banks are still geothermally influenced and therefore are not covered with snow to the same depth as the surrounding country. Bison gather around the pond because of its relatively snow-free character.

A mile or so beyond Indian Pond is Mary Bay, a much larger steam explosion crater. Thermal activity on the west end of Mary Bay, in an area known as Beach Springs, is obvious and sometimes the cause of bare pavement on the road. There are lots of bison here, too. You will also have the chance to see trumpeter swans and others in or around breather holes kept open in the ice by offshore geothermal vents.

Beyond Mary Bay is Steamboat Point. Thermal activity and the windswept nature of the point are often the cause of bare pavement here as well. Remember that snowmobiles tend to drift downhill when driven over pavement, so be careful. There are more breather holes offshore from Steamboat Point, and Canada geese are often seen around these. The road around Steamboat Point hangs high on the side of a steep bluff, so you get to see whatever birds or animals are present around the open water from an unusual, overhead perspective.

Sedge Bay and Butte Springs are east of Steamboat. You'll probably see more bull bison around the springs and have a good view of the country south of Yellowstone Lake.

East of Sedge Bay the road begins its ascent to Sylvan Pass, 8,557 feet high and an 800-foot vertical climb from the elevation of Yellowstone Lake. Sylvan Pass is notched between stupendous cliffs from which avalanches sometimes descend. The peaks in the vicinity have colorful names such as Top Notch, Grizzly, and Avalanche. A good view of Top Notch Peak can be had across Sylvan Lake, which will appear on the south side of the road. From Sylvan Lake it's easy to see how Top Notch Peak got its name.

From Sylvan Pass the road descends steeply toward East Entrance. Middle Creek and Sylvan Meadows will appear as snowy bottomland on your right. The precipitous peaks you can see ahead of you are mostly outside Yellowstone Park. Crow Peak, Whirlwind Peak, and Sleeping Giant Mountain are three of the mountains you'll be able to see if the weather is clear. They are all in the Shoshone National Forest.

East Entrance is about 26 miles from Fishing Bridge. Pahaska Teepee is 2 miles farther down the road toward Cody, Wyoming. These 2 miles are snowpacked, so you can snowmobile all the way to the resort.

Pahaska Teepee means Long Hair's Lodge in the Sioux Indian tongue. It was Buffalo Bill Cody's hunting lodge in the early twentieth century and the name was given to the place by some of his Sioux friends. The resort offers fuel, food, lodging, a gift shop, and snowmobile and cross country ski rentals. The town of Cody is about 52 more miles east. The road from Pahaska Teepee to Cody is plowed and maintained for wheeled vehicles. The address is Pahaska Teepee Resort, Wapiti, Wyoming 82450, telephone (307) 527-7701.

WEST THUMB TO SOUTH ENTRANCE/FLAGG RANCH (22 MILES OVERSNOW)

The first 2 miles of road south from West Thumb pass through an intermittent thermal area. Occasionally elk, moose, and bison are seen in and around these thermal openings. A good view of frozen Yellowstone Lake and the Absaroka Mountains to the east is possible from the bridge over Big Thumb Creek, about 2 miles south of West Thumb Junction. This will be your last view of the lake and the Absarokas on your trip to South Entrance.

The road continues south past Grant Village, all closed in the winter, crossing the Continental Divide about 3 miles south of Grant Village Junction. This crossing will put you on the west side of the divide, in the drainage of the Pacific Ocean. The country is high (8,000–8,500 feet) and mostly forested with lodgepole pine, Engelmann spruce, and subalpine fir. Because of its high elevation and lack of geothermal influence this area is not suitable winter habitat for large mammals, and sightings are rare.

Three to 4 miles south of the Continental Divide you'll come to Lewis Lake, which will appear as a large expanse of ice to the west. Lewis Lake and Lewis River, which flows both into and out of the lake, are names that date back to the days of the Lewis and Clark Expedition. Meriwether Lewis and William Clark and their Corps of Discovery never came through this area, but they did travel the Snake River system farther downstream in present-day Idaho. For a time in the

JIM MCBRIDE AND STEVE BLAKELEY REMOVING SNOW FROM ROOF OF LAKE LODGE

nineteenth century the entire Snake River carried Lewis's name. The current Lewis River preserves the name and is a tributary of the larger Snake. You may see some steam from geothermal activity on the far side of Lewis Lake.

South of Lewis Lake is Lewis Falls, where the river of the same name forms a lovely cascade. The falls can be viewed from turnouts at either end of the bridge over the river.

The road parallels Lewis River for a couple of miles before the river descends into the Lewis Canyon. You'll have good views of the canyon from your choice of several roadside turnouts a few miles south of where the river and the road part ways.

Turning away from Lewis Canyon; the road to South Entrance enters what some people call the Teton Straightaway. That's because the road is straight and the Teton Mountains are in sight to the south, straight ahead of you. The road here is decidedly downhill, too, beginning its descent from the high Yellowstone plateau country to Jackson's Hole. A few miles more and you'll arrive at South Entrance, where National Park Service rangers can answer questions or, if necessary, render assistance. Two more miles of snowmobiling will bring you to Flagg Ranch, the end of the road for oversnow travel. From here to Jackson, Wyoming (55 miles south), the road is plowed and maintained for wheeled vehicles. Flagg Ranch has fuel, snowmobile and cross country ski rentals, food, lodging, and other services. Its address is Flagg Ranch, Moran, Wyoming 83013, telephone (307) 543-2861 or 733-8761. The latter number is a local call from the town of Jackson.

NORRIS TO MAMMOTH HOT SPRINGS (21 MILES OVERSNOW)

From Norris Junction your route toward Mammoth will take you over the Gibbon River; through the northeast corner of the Norris Geyser Basin, where you will encounter at least some bare pavement; and past Nymph Lake, a geothermal body of water to the west of the road. There is a good possibility that you will see cow and young elk somewhere along this stretch of road.

About 5 miles north of Norris you'll come to Roaring Mountain, on the east side of the road. This is a collection of noisy steam vents on the side of a hill. If you stop and turn off your machine you'll understand how the feature got its name, although the roar of Roaring Mountain is reputedly not as loud as it used to be. The burned trees around Roaring Mountain are a legacy of the 1988 North Fork Fire, which burned intermittently all along the road from Norris to Mammoth.

Obsidian Creek will be on your left as you leave Roaring Mountain. This thermal stream will be open regardless of how cold the weather has been, and you undoubtedly will see elk somewhere along its course. You may see some bull bison along Obsidian Creek, too.

Obsidian Cliff will soon appear on your right. Because of snow cover you may not be able to see any of the black volcanic glass from which Obsidian Cliff gets its name, but you can stop and read the interpretive display across the road from the cliff. If you do, you'll learn that this feature was the "Mountain of Glass" in early trapper tales and the source of raw material for native American tools and projectile points that have been located as far away as Ohio. A few miles beyond Obsidian Cliff you'll pass Appollinaris Spring, whose waters supposedly taste much like those from a spring of the same name in Germany.

Soon you'll cross the Gardner River, pass through a semi-open lodgepole pine forest, and then break out of the woods onto Swan Lake Flat. The flat is part of what the mountain men of the early nineteenth century called Gardner's Hole, named for one Johnson Gardner, a prominent trapper and mountain man. If you look closely around the windswept slopes above Swan Lake Flat, you should be able to spot a few large bull elk. The mountain with the sharp peak northwest of you is Electric Peak. It's 10,992 feet high and a part of the Gallatin Mountain Range. Other peaks in this range can be seen to the west.

On the north side of Gardner's Hole you'll pass through a notch between Terrace Mountain on the west and Bunsen Peak on the east and begin a steep descent toward Mammoth Hot Springs. The notch is known as Kingman Pass, the stream that flows through it is Glen Creek, and the beautiful ice cone on the right side of the road marks what is called Rustic Falls.

The road through this windy pass is apt to be bare of snow, so it will pay to cut your speed and use caution as you descend. The National Park Service spreads wood chips on this stretch of road in late fall, as it does on other stretches of road where wind and thermal activity tend to keep the pavement snow-free. The wood chips are a great idea—snowmobiles and snowcoaches handle quite well on them—but some patches of bare pavement are inevitable and have to be negotiated.

Past Kingman Pass you'll start to see a few aspen trees as the vegetation begins to change with your drop in elevation. You'll also pass through the Hoodoos, a weird assemblage of boulders that actually are just coarse detritus from Terrace Mountain, the rim of which can be seen higher up the slope. Mule deer are sometimes seen around the Hoodoos. On a clear day you'll be able to see large mountain peaks to the north. Sheep Mountain is the most apparent of these. It's due north of the town of Gardiner, Montana, outside Yellowstone National Park in the Gallatin National Forest.

Signs and a brace of blinking red lights soon will warn you that you are coming to the end of the snowmobile road. There is a snowmobile rental hut on the lower, or right-hand, side of the road at this point. It's operated by Amfac Parks and Resorts, Yellowstone, which sells gasoline and other snowmobile supplies in conjunction with its snow-mobile rental business. Perhaps more important if you've snowmobiled from somewhere else, a frequent shuttle service runs between the hut and Mammoth Hot Springs Hotel, about 2 miles down the hill. The hotel has a fast food outlet, a restaurant, a gift shop, overnight lodging, and other services. A Hamilton's General Store and a National Park Service Visitor Center are also open in the Mammoth area during the winter. The town of Gardiner, Montana, is 5 miles down the hill from Mammoth.

GARDINER TO COOKE CITY
(55 MILES, WHEELED VEHICLES ONLY)

At the North Entrance Station at Gardiner, Montana, you will be charged a $20-per-vehicle entry fee and given a packet of information about the park. Holders of Golden Age, Golden Access, or Golden Eagle Passports may enter the park free of charge. The attendant on duty in the entrance booth can answer your questions about these passports and other matters.

Already you may have seen elk when you drove through the town of Gardiner, and you undoubtedly will see some soon after you pass through the park gate. Mule deer and pronghorn antelope also fre-quent the flats around the park boundary. In some winters you may see bison here, too. In Yellowstone the direction north means down, which means the northern tier of the park is lower in elevation. Therefore this area is critical winter range for a significant percentage of Yellowstone's large mammals.

A mile and a half inside North Gate you'll enter the lower end of the Gardiner River Canyon. The steep slopes of the canyon, especially on the east, or left-hand, side of the road, are a winter home to bighorn sheep; if you look closely, perhaps with binoculars, you'll probably see a few sheep. Be advised that parts of this area are closed to foot travel during the winter to minimize human impact on the sheep. It's best to check with a ranger before hiking into the sheep range. If you are for-tunate enough to spot sheep in the canyon, be sure not to stop and look until you've pulled off in one of the several pullouts in the area—this stretch of road gets a lot of traffic.

Above Gardiner Canyon you'll come to a riverside flat known as the Chinese Garden. Chinese cooks from Mammoth used to grow vegeta-bles here to feed the U.S. Army soldiers who protected Yellowstone in the days before the National Park Service had been created. Mule deer and elk now use the flat for winter range.

Just upstream from the Chinese Garden is the 45th parallel of latitude, halfway between the equator and the North Pole. From here the road begins to climb steeply, winds around some S-curves, and then straightens out on a grade known as Soap Hill. The hill got its name in the days of horses and stagecoaches and unpaved roads, when rain could make the hill slick as soap. Snow or ice on the road nowadays can make it just as slick.

At Mammoth you'll find the National Park Service's Horace Albright Visitor Center, which offers an information desk, book sales, and a museum. You'll also find a Hamilton's General Store open for winter business and the Mammoth Hot Springs Hotel. The hotel has a fast food outlet, a restaurant, a gift shop, snowmobile rentals (for use on the roads south of Mammoth, in the park's interior), lodging, and other services. The hotel is operated by Amfac Parks and Resorts.

SNOWMOBILERS CARRIE HOLDER AND DIANE HILBORN AT SWAN LAKE FLAT

In front of Mammoth Hotel is a road junction. Continuing straight through the junction will take you 2 miles to the point where the plowed road ends and the groomed snowmobile road commences. You may want to take this fork for a look at the Mammoth Hot Springs Terraces. Always remarkable, the terraces are doubly dramatic in the cold air and shifting steam clouds of winter. Boardwalks and interpretive pamphlets (25¢) are available if you're inclined to take a walk.

Returning to Mammoth and turning east at the intersection will put you on the road to Tower Junction. At the point where you leave the Mammoth developed area, you'll cross the steaming runoff channel from the Mammoth Terraces. You almost certainly will see female and young elk somewhere around the stream.

Another mile or so and you will cross the Gardner River—the same stream you followed from the town of Gardiner to Mammoth Hot Springs—and begin a steep ascent. At the top of this rise (2.5 miles or so) the road levels off at the Undine Falls turnout. The next 2 miles of country burned in September 1988 but is still an excellent area to find mature bull elk. These striking animals are often seen around the road crossing of Lava Creek and around the Wraith Falls trailhead. For some reason bull elk are particularly loyal to their winter ranges, and this area has been a wintering ground for generations of bulls, a fact that did not change after the 1988 fire.

Beyond the Wraith Falls trailhead the road traverses a long flat, passing Blacktail Ponds on the left (north) before crossing Blacktail Creek. East of Blacktail Creek the road climbs onto Blacktail Plateau. The declivity to the north leads down to the Black Canyon of the Yellowstone River; much of the high country you can see to the north of the canyon is outside the park in the Absaroka-Beartooth Wilderness Area.

If you are travelling across Blacktail Plateau in early winter or during a mild, dry winter, you may see large numbers of elk. Blacktail is a transitional zone between summer and winter ranges. Elk pass through here on their way to lower elevations farther north and seemingly have a tendency to linger on the plateau as long as the weather and snow depths permit.

Continuing east 1.5 miles beyond Blacktail Creek, you will come to a large parking lot on your right. The area is plowed so skiers can park their cars and ski the Blacktail Plateau trail, the western end of which is at the edge of the parking area. Just east of the parking lot and near the main road rests a large boulder by a thin stand of lodgepole pines. This is called Frog Rock, though many people have trouble making out the resemblance between the rock and a frog.

Curves and ups and downs characterize the road east of Frog Rock. The orientation of this stretch of road is primarily north-facing, so it's apt to be icy. It's possible to see elk, mostly cows and young in small groups, just about anywhere along this sector. Somewhere you'll see coyotes, too. And somewhere between Gardiner and Lamar Valley you'll see bison. The movements of the bison herd in northern Yellowstone are more unpredictable than those of herds elsewhere in the park, and this has been especially true in recent years. It is safe to say that you'll have at least a fair chance of seeing some bison around Phantom Lake (marked with a brown and white park sign) or around the headwaters of Geode and Oxbow Creeks (you'll have to locate these on a map, as they are not marked).

SNOWMOBILER
KATHY SUCHER ON
PARK ROAD AT
SWAN LAKE FLAT

About 1.5 miles beyond Geode and Oxbow Creeks, you'll come to the Hellroaring Overlook, a turnout on the north (left) side of the road. From here you can see into the Black Canyon of the Yellowstone below and to Hellroaring Creek beyond. The horizon line to the north is pretty close to the boundary between Yellowstone National Park and the Absaroka-Beartooth Wilderness. With binoculars or a telescope you can scan the Hellroaring slopes to the east of the creek for wildlife. You'll see at least some elk—and probably some bison, too.

The lower reaches of the slopes will be more snow-free than you might expect. That's because of their lower elevation and their south-facing aspect. Using binoculars or telescopes to spot animals as large as elk and bison and then realizing how tiny they appear even when magnified will help you appreciate the immensity of the space in front of you at Hellroaring Overlook.

From here the Mammoth-Tower road descends steeply to a meadow above one of the trailheads into the Hellroaring country. Beyond the trailhead the road passes Floating Island Lake, where elk tracks on the ice make interesting patterns. A short distance past the lake you'll be able to see into Pleasant Valley on your left. This is another prime wintering ground for large bull elk, and somewhere between here and Tower Junction you will see some. You have a good chance of seeing some bison hereabouts, too.

Tower Junction is the hub of several popular cross country ski trails (see chapter 8 for more information). You'll probably see some skiers and certainly their parked cars at the end of the road that leads to Dunraven Pass and Canyon. That road obviously is closed to cars in winter, and it's closed to snowmobiles, too. Most people who ski the road go only to Tower Falls (about 3 miles) or a little farther. If you are an energetic, good skier and wish to ski up to Dunraven Pass (about 12 miles to the top of the pass) or beyond, you should check with a park ranger on snow and avalanche conditions in the higher country. There's a ranger station about a quarter mile west of the junction, on the road back toward Mammoth.

Turning left at Tower Junction will put you on the road to Cooke City, Montana. It's 32 miles to Cooke, which is 4 miles beyond the Northeast Gate to Yellowstone Park.

A mile or so east of Tower you'll cross the Yellowstone River. Here you'll have a look at the jagged volcanic walls forming the head of the Black Canyon. They're even more impressive a little way downstream in the canyon proper.

After winding around a big curve above the bridge, you'll pass

Junction Butte on your left. Then you'll cross Little America Flats with its collection of glacial ponds and boulders. This is a great place to see coyotes. There probably will be elk—cows and young—in the neighborhood as well. The toothlike crags you can see to the northeast up the Slough Creek Valley form Cutoff Mountain, which is 10,300 feet high.

Specimen Ridge will be on your right (south) and Lamar River on your left as you cross a long flat. Sightings of coyotes, bison, and elk are all possibilities along this stretch. At the end of the flat—about 5 miles from Tower Junction—you will cross over the Lamar River. Turnouts at the bridge offer a good chance of spotting bull elk upslope to the south, in the drainage of Crystal Creek.

Beyond the Lamar crossing the road passes the turnoff to Slough Creek, on the left side of the highway. This road is closed to traffic in winter and is another popular ski trail. Next you'll enter Lamar Canyon, where there's a chance of seeing a mule deer or two on the uphill (left) side of the road.

When you exit the canyon at its upper end, you'll be greeted by what mountain man Osborne Russel in 1834 described as "a beautiful valley about eight mls. long and three or four wide surrounded by dark and lofty mountains." Other, more recent observers have described Lamar Valley as the "Serengeti of North America." The latter description is most fitting in winter, when large herds of ungulates, particularly elk, gather there to spend the cold months. You'll certainly see at least some bison, coyotes, and elk—perhaps large numbers of the last—in the expanse of the valley. You also will see some waterfowl and possibly some otters along the river at the upstream, or eastern, end of the valley. About 3 miles east of Lamar Canyon is a ranger station where you can go for emergency assistance.

At the eastern end of Lamar Valley is the mouth of Soda Butte Creek. Immediately north and above the road at this point is an old roadbed (you'll have to look closely to see it) known as Jackson Grade. This area is a perennial wintering ground for a small band of bighorn sheep. The sheep are always around in winter, and if you look for them long enough you'll probably spot them. Sometimes the sheep are out of sight in the timber upslope, and if you tire of looking but really would like to see them, you can always look again when you return from Cooke City. The bighorns have made a good choice for their winter home: It faces south, so the snow doesn't accumulate as deeply there as elsewhere. Please don't disturb the sheep by climbing amongst them.

Two miles from Jackson Grade is Soda Butte. It's a peculiar hydrothermal deposit that some people think looks like a giant's hat resting on the ground. The area near the butte is a good place to spot bull bison in winter. It's also a good place to spot coyotes. The unpleasant odor that may be present is from some hot springs that issue from the ground on the flat beyond Soda Butte.

Beyond Soda Butte are Round Prairie and the mouth of Pebble Creek. By now you'll be among huge mountain peaks. Mount Norris, the Thunderer, Abiathar Peak, and Barronette Peak are some you will see. You will need a map to sort them out if you have the time and the interest.

Northeast Entrance is about 10 more miles up Soda Butte Creek; the valley continually narrows and steepens as you go on. You climb in elevation, too, and the snow depth along the sides of the road deepens accordingly. You'll know Northeast Gate when you get there—it's an attractive log structure. Again, you can procure emergency assistance here if you need it. Remember, too, that help can be reached by dialing 9-1-1 from any telephone in Yellowstone National Park.

Silver Gate and Cooke City, Montana, are respectively 2 and 4 miles outside the park. They are the places to go for cross country skiing and snowmobiling in spectacular mountain country. Rentals, fuel, lodging, and food are all available, especially in Cooke City, the larger of the two communities. The plowed road ends at the east end of Cooke City, so unless you want to snowmobile over the Beartooth Pass—which is a possibility for those who want to do so—you'll have to return to Gardiner through Yellowstone National Park. Lists of businesses offering services in Cooke City and Silver Gate are found elsewhere in this book: Lodging businesses are found at the end of chapter 4, and snowmobile rental outlets are listed at the end of chapter 5.

SNOWCOACH WITH
WINTER VISITORS
PHOTOGRAPHING
WILDLIFE

Skiing and Snowshoeing

Unique scenery, geysers, wildlife, relatively flat terrain, lots of fluffy powder snow—these are some of the reasons Yellowstone is known far and wide as a mecca for cross country skiers. Skiing conditions are so good that the United States cross country and biathlon teams annually gather in West Yellowstone, Montana, to take advantage of the area's early winter and reliable snowfall.

Cross country skiing in Yellowstone dates back to the days when the U.S. Cavalry protected the park (1886–1916), before the establishment of the National Park Service. Troopers of that era quickly decided winter patrol was much easier on skis than on snowshoes—even though the skis they used were long wooden creations weighing about ten pounds apiece. The soldiers propelled and balanced themselves through the use of a single pole.

Equipment has improved dramatically since then, and today's skier may choose from skis of many different styles and compositions, all

SKIERS ON UPPER TERRACE DRIVE, MAMMOTH HOT SPRINGS

weighing considerably less than ten pounds apiece. There are designs for all levels of ability, for the different styles of Nordic skiing, and for various snow conditions.

One of the many beauties of cross country skiing is that a rank novice can, with just a few hours of instruction and practice, reach a point where he or she can shuffle around on the level and even negotiate slight grades. With interest and practice, a person can continue to develop Nordic skills through an entire lifetime. That's another beauty of the spoil: While it's one of the best all-around exercises, its gentle, gliding motion doesn't wear and tear on the body, so it can be pursued until a fairly advanced age. Skiers in their sixties and seventies are seen every winter in Yellowstone.

You can rent skis at Amfac Parks and Resorts' ski shops at Old Faithful Snow Lodge and at Mammoth Hot Springs Hotel. Each shop is known as the Bear Den and each offers equipment sales as well as rentals. Two-hour group lessons are also available at appointed times, one in the morning and another in the afternoon. Private lessons are available by reservation. The Bear Dens are staffed by truly exceptional cross country skiers who are good people to talk to for advice or trail conditions, even if you don't need lessons or equipment.

Amfac also provides dropoff services for skiers from Old Faithful and Mammoth. Snowcoaches regularly ferry skiers from Old Faithful to the Divide Lookout and Fairy Falls trailheads (see the ski map for the Old Faithful area at the end of chapter 8). Pickups and dropoffs to more out-of-the-way places can be arranged. A daylong snowcoach excursion from Old Faithful to Canyon combined with a ski tour of the Canyon area is also available on a daily basis. A shuttle van takes skiers from the Mammoth Hotel to drop points along the Tower-Mammoth road. Regularly scheduled pickups are made along the same road. A snowcoach makes regular runs from Mammoth to drop skiers along the road toward Norris as far out as Indian Creek. Pickups are possible along the same stretch, but skiers dropped there often choose to ski all the way back to Mammoth because a good portion of the trip is downhill. You can also take a coach from Mammoth to Canyon for a daylong ski tour of that area. Maps at the end of chapter 8 illustrate the ski trails in the Mammoth, Tower, and Canyon areas. These ski maps were furnished through the courtesy of the U.S. National Park Service in Yellowstone National Park.

Most of Yellowstone Park is a high plateau with relatively flat terrain. You may question this statement when you're chugging up a hill or screaming down one while skiing in the park, but if you think back to some of the country you passed through just before you got to Yellowstone—places such as the Gallatin Canyon or the Teton Mountain Range—you'll realize that it is true. The gradual grades of the park interior lend themselves to cross country skiing, and the high elevation of the Yellowstone plateau country accounts for the usually plentiful snowfall.

The high elevation also accounts for two other phenomena that have to be reckoned with: cold weather and thin air. If you're like almost everybody else in North America, you come from an area that is lower in elevation than Yellowstone National Park, most of which is 7,000–9,000 feet above sea level, and your body will not be acclimated to this altitude. You probably will tire more quickly under exertion than you would at home; even the best conditioned athletes can feel the difference. People at high elevations dehydrate more quickly, too, a problem that can sneak up on you in cold weather, when thirst doesn't strike as readily as it does when you're hot. You should carry water or juice with you when you ski and force yourself to drink even if you don't feel thirsty.

Winter weather often changes quickly in the Yellowstone high country and conditions sometimes become severe. Many authors have pointed out that a day that begins warm and sunny can end in a howling blizzard with plummeting temperatures. Likewise, a skier pumping along in light clothing may be warm from exertion but will chill quickly if halted by equipment failure or injury. In short, it pays to be prepared by carrying extra clothing, food, and matches. A basic first aid kit and stuff to effect emergency repairs on your ski equipment are also recommended. Of course, having a first aid kit isn't much good if no one in your group has some knowledge of first aid. Duct tape, a spare bale for your ski bindings, and a temporary replacement tip for a broken ski are important pieces of repair gear that might save you a long walk through deep snow, a walk that in some snow conditions might not even be possible.

Now for equipment information: Cross country touring skis come in two basic types, waxless and waxable. Waxless skis have bottom surfaces modeled after a fish's scales so that they slide forward over the snow but not back. Waxless skis are generally more hassle-free than waxed skis and are considered easier for the beginner to use. Another advantage becomes apparent in the late winter and spring, when varied and rapidly changing snow conditions make for difficult, if not impossible, waxing situations. The chief drawback of waxless skis is that they are much slower than waxed models.

Using waxed skis is a little more involved but probably not as complicated as you think. All skis, even waxless ones, are treated with a base or glider wax. This helps the ski to glide through and over the snow more easily, much as a waxed dust cloth slides easily over a piece of hardwood furniture. The base wax helps prevent snow and ice buildup on the bottom of the ski, too.

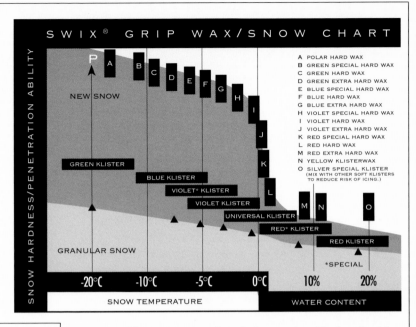

S W I X® G R I P W A X / S N O W C H A R T

SNOW HARDNESS/PENETRATION ABILITY

NEW SNOW

GREEN KLISTER

BLUE KLISTER

VIOLET* KLISTER

VIOLET KLISTER

UNIVERSAL KLISTER

RED* KLISTER

RED KLISTER

GRANULAR SNOW

*SPECIAL

A POLAR HARD WAX
B GREEN SPECIAL HARD WAX
C GREEN HARD WAX
D GREEN EXTRA HARD WAX
E BLUE SPECIAL HARD WAX
F BLUE HARD WAX
G BLUE EXTRA HARD WAX
H VIOLET SPECIAL HARD WAX
I VIOLET HARD WAX
J VIOLET EXTRA HARD WAX
K RED SPECIAL HARD WAX
L RED HARD WAX
M RED EXTRA HARD WAX
N YELLOW KLISTERWAX
O SILVER SPECIAL KLISTER
   (MIX WITH OTHER SOFT KLISTERS
   TO REDUCE RISK OF ICING.)

-20°C   -10°C   -5°C   0°C   10%   20%

SNOW TEMPERATURE   WATER CONTENT

ADAPTED FROM A
SWIX COLOR
CHART, COURTESY
OF SWIX SPORT
USA

On waxable cross country skis a kicker wax is rubbed on the ski on top of the glider wax. The kicker wax is applied to an approximately two- to four-foot section of the ski, the waxed area being centered under the ski's binding. The kicker wax gives traction for the skier's thrust but miraculously does not impede the ski's forward glide—that is, it does not if you apply the proper wax for the existing temperature and snow conditions.

The gliding properties of snow vary according to its crystalline structure and its ambient temperature, with warmer snow generally being more slippery than cold snow. Kicker waxes are available in varying viscosities to match various snow conditions. Choosing the correct wax is not as tough as it sounds, because the waxes are color-coded according to their temperature ranges. In addition, wax manufacturers provide information as to which colors to use in given situations on the tubes the waxes come in and on charts that are freely distributed to the public. You'll notice on the Swix Company's wax chart (above) that there are two families of kicker waxes: hard waxes for fresh snow and klister waxes designed for use in old, coarse-grained snow. Old snow on the surface of the snowpack is a phenomenon usually not seen in Yellowstone until late winter or spring, so unless you're here at that time you probably won't have to worry about klisters. Even if you do need to use a klister, just read the temperature guidelines and wax accordingly. The guidelines aren't correct 100 percent of the time—snow is an infinitely varied and dynamic substance—but they are a good place to start.

As you develop as a cross country skier you will become better at fine-tuning your waxing strategies.

An additional tip about waxing: You can apply a warmer wax over a colder wax but not the other way around. Therefore, it pays to wax a little on the cold side when you start your day, especially if you're beginning your ski in the morning, when temperatures are presumably cooler than they will be at midday. If you do wax too warm, which means you will stick to the snow when you're trying to glide, you will have to scrape off the warm kicker wax and start over. To do that you'll need a ski scraper, a handy palm-size tool that costs about $5. Another valuable accessory is a waxing cork, used to smooth out lumps in your kicker wax after you've rubbed it on your ski. This also costs around $5.

Even before you worry about waxing, you will have to find skis and poles of the proper size. The general rule of thumb for selecting a ski length is that the upright ski should reach to your wrist when your arm is stretched straight above your head. Poles for touring should come about to your armpits. These are general guidelines; there's a lot more to cross country skiing than there is space to cover here. Two books that discuss Nordic skiing in depth are *Cross Country Skiing* by Sindre Bergan and Bob O'Connor and *Cross Country Skiing: A Complete Guide* by Brian Cazeneuve. If you really get enthused about cross country skiing, your interest can take you from there.

Regardless of your level of ability, geothermal features and wildlife are two elements that will make skiing in Yellowstone a unique experience. Where else can you tour through bubbling hot springs and spouting geysers in sight of wintering bison and elk? These features are especially apparent for skiers in the Old Faithful area, where practically every trail leads through some thermal activity and winter wildlife range. There are several points to bear in mind about skiing in geyser basins. One is that geothermal heat in some places creates snow-free stretches of ski trail. Some of these barren areas are only a few feet wide, but in dry years and in late winter some grow to be quite large. In the latter case it usually makes sense to remove your skis and walk. A ski binder of some type, such as a rubber band, a spare shoestring, or a commercially produced ski clasp, is useful here; skis are much easier to carry when they are tied together. If you decide to cross a thermal plain without taking your skis off, remember to lift and place your steps carefully. Sliding or shuffling your skis over bare dirt and gravel will worsen the gouging on your skis.

In some places hydrothermal spray and mist fall and freeze on ski trails. The boardwalk a few feet north of Castle Geyser in the Upper Geyser Basin is a good example of this phenomenon. Where this happens, a deep and hard ice pack can develop, a situation where cross country skis can be worse than useless. Removing your skis and taking care to dig in your boot heels as you walk across these icy stretches is a good idea. A slip on such places can mean a fall of six feet or more from a snow- and ice-covered boardwalk to bare thermal earth below. At worst, a slip could land a person in a boiling spring.

Around Old Faithful you will certainly encounter wildlife, especially elk and bison. For fear of provoking a confrontation or of unduly stressing these animals, you should maintain a good space cushion between them and you. National Park Service regulations say you should approach no closer than 25 yards. It's possible to appreciate the wildlife and to make memorable photographs of them from a respectful distance. Remember that conserving energy is a matter of life and death for these animals in winter.

COYOTE TRACKS AT
SUNRISE, ALUM
CREEK, HAYDEN
VALLEY

You'll also have a good chance of seeing coyotes and mule deer in the geyser basins. The deer are a small group, varying from about six to eighteen in number, and they are distinctive for possibly being the only deer that winter in the central Yellowstone National Park. They and their ancestors have wintered in the area between Old Faithful and Biscuit Basin for as long as such things have been recorded.

Coyotes in the geyser basins have been cause for some concern of late. One coyote attacked a lone skier in Biscuit Basin (a few miles north of Old Faithful) in January 1990. Reasons for this highly unusual attack are not totally clear, but the coyote probably had become accustomed to people and possibly to their food over a period of time. Skiing in a group will further minimize the extremely remote possibility of another attack.

COYOTE TRAVELS ALONG ALUM CREEK, HAYDEN VALLEY

Skiers in northern Yellowstone National Park won't come across nearly as much geothermal activity as those in the Old Faithful area. They won't encounter as much wildlife in close proximity, either, even though in total numbers wildlife populations (especially elk populations) on the Northern Range exceed those of the Firehole River geyser basins. Without exaggeration, skiers up north may see thousands of elk in a single day tour, but the elk for the most part will keep their distance. That's because the elk of Yellowstone's northern herd seasonally migrate outside the park, where they are legally hunted in the state of Montana, and therefore tend to be more wary of humans. The exceptions, of course, are the elk at Mammoth Hot Springs. Those animals spend virtually the entire year feeding on the rich grass of Mammoth's fertilized lawns and are very accustomed to people.

Here are some differences between skiing around Old Faithful and skiing Yellowstone's northern tier. The skiers up north:

▲   will see some but not as many bison,

▲   will see more mule deer,

▲   may see some bighorn sheep,

▲   may see more coyotes,

▲   will encounter more hills and open country,

▲   will encounter less snow (because of lower elevations),

▲   will enjoy more expansive vistas.

The principal attractions of skiing around Canyon are the quantity (lots) and quality (great) of the snow found there and the spectacular views of the Upper and Lower Falls and of the Grand Canyon of the Yellowstone River. Skiers at Canyon will see some wildlife, mostly large bull bison and possibly a coyote or two, but not nearly as much as is found around Old Faithful on Yellowstone's Northern Range.

SNOWSHOEING

In recent years snowshoeing has gained great popularity as an alternative to cross country skiing, perhaps because of the perception that snowshoeing requires less skill and is less dangerous than skiing. Probably true, but this doesn't mean that snowshoeing is necessarily easy. It can be quite taxing, especially if the snow is deep and powdery.

Snowshoes are made from various materials and come in a great variety of sizes and designs. All designs involve a perimeter framework—basically an oblong hoop—across which coarse lacing is woven to support a person's foot above the snow. This webbing displaces the person's weight over a greater expanse of snow and this prevents "postholing," where the foot sinks into the snow until it hits the ground or the crotch hits the snow, whichever comes first. Bindings of various types hold the foot and snowshoe together.

Most snowshoes are either round tailed or long tailed: Round-tailed shoes are rounded at the heel while long-tailed designs are tapered to a pointed tip. Generally, the rounded-heel varieties work better in hilly country like Yellowstone, preventing the user from sliding backward on uphill grades. Tapered tails perform better in flat, brushy country—much of Minnesota, for example—where a user doesn't have to worry about upgrades and where the feathered heels shed tangling undergrowth. Both styles have slightly upturned toes to prevent tripping on the forestep. Neither style should be used to span a gap such as a low spot in the ground, a rivulet, or a space between fallen logs. Snowshoes aren't designed for such "bridging," and are apt to break if so misused. Ski poles are handy accessories for any type of snowshoes.

Traditionally, snowshoes were made with wooden frames and rawhide webbing. Modern versions are usually aluminum framed and laced with synthetic cords. Many people find the original wood and rawhide varieties more aesthetically pleasing, while contemporary models are cheaper to buy and much easier to maintain.

Snowshoes have an interesting history. For many thousands of years they were native North Americans' solution to the problem of traveling through deep snow, a problem that northern Europeans solved by the evolution of the ski. The snowshoe and the ski offer a fascinating contrast as two very different solutions to a very similar problem. To learn more about snowshoes, a good source is *The Snowshoe Book* by William Osgood and Leslie Hurley.

PARK VISITORS WITH RENTED SNOWSHOES, UPPER GEYSER BASIN

The Bear Den ski shops at Old Faithful Snow Lodge and at Mammoth Hot Springs Hotel offer snowshoe rentals as well as guided snowshoe tours. Rental 'shoes are available for either half days or full days and rental fees are reasonable. Guided tours in the Old Faithful area usually take in the Upper Geyser Basin as well as Observation Point, where snowshoers can enjoy a fine overview of Old Faithful Geyser and the surrounding area. Tours in the Mammoth area begin in the vicinity of the Mammoth Hot Springs Terraces and wind uphill from there through aspen and Douglas fir forests. Visitors in both areas are almost certain to see some large wild animals on their tours, including elk and bison at Old Faithful and elk and probably mule deer at Mammoth.

Additional sightings of other wildlife species are likely in both areas. In all areas, snowshoers should avoid using designated ski trails. Snowshoes tramp out ski tracks, and snowshoers usually move at much slower speeds than do skiers.

In some parts of the country, snowboarders use snowshoes to hike up hills or ridges, from which they snowboard down with their snowshoes lashed to their backs. This hasn't happened very much in Yellowstone, at least not yet, and generally snowboarding in the park is almost unheard of. Lack of easy access to snowboarding terrain is probably the biggest reason for snowboarding's absence. The remoteness of suitable snowboarding terrain would necessitate a long, cold snowmobile ride at the end of the day. Perhaps most would-be snowboarders are discouraged by the thought of such a ride, especially when they consider how wet one can get from perspiration and flying snow when pursuing their sport.

BACKCOUNTRY SKIING

Backcountry skiing is popular in Yellowstone, perhaps more so than ever. People ski the backcountry to see areas not accessible by road and to escape the commotion of the front country. Understandable desires, but I should point out here that in Yellowstone National Park's history at least seventeen people have died from hypothermia or as a result of avalanches.

By its very nature, backcountry travel requires some level of self-reliance. The backcountry traveler should carry (as a minimum) the survival and repair items listed earlier in this chapter. For travel in remote areas, a compass, a map of the local area, and a knowledge of navigation should be added to the list. Global positioning system units work in Yellowstone and could be useful on backcountry ski or snowshoe trips.

Avalanches are a constant threat during Yellowstone's winter season. One person was killed by an avalanche in the park in 1992 and two more died in an avalanche in 1997. All three were park employees; two of them were good friends. My two friends were good outdoorsmen and were very experienced in Yellowstone, illustrating that avalanches are often difficult to predict.

Avalanches—masses of snow that fracture and rush down slopes—can be released by many possible triggers: new snow, windblown snow, other weather factors, the impact of a skier or snowshoer, an animal, or in an unusual example, simply the sound of a human voice. I saw the latter happen once at Old Faithful, when a woman's shout to her companions triggered a 200-foot-wide slide off the roof of the Old Faithful Inn. The woman and her companions were out of harm's way, but I found the incident very revealing.

Also revealing was an incident in 1993 when five friends and I were clearing snow from the roof of another building at Old Faithful. The roof unexpectedly avalanched on us—something I had always thought impossible because of the bracing of the snowpack provided on this particular roof by a series of dormers and valleys. The avalanche carried four of us off the roof and we landed on top of the snow. But the other two were buried, one to his waist and the other to his neck. The four of us who were free had no trouble digging out the two who were stuck, but the revealing part—in addition to the fact that the roof avalanched at all—was how fast the avalanche debris had set up. Even after we had dug down to the tops of their boots, the two men still couldn't pull their feet free without an additional shovel plant and pry. This roof avalanche was small compared to hillsides and mountain slopes where natural and triggered slides occur.

A person caught in a backcountry avalanche is in dire jeopardy. If not crushed in the churning snow and debris in the initial rush, a victim is quite apt to wind up buried in the avalanche debris, and death by suffocation usually follows quite quickly.

The only way to be completely safe from avalanche danger is to avoid avalanche country during winter. Many recreationists are unwilling to do that, however, and if you plan to travel in the backcountry it behooves you to learn as much as possible about avalanches. It also pays to invest in avalanche safety equipment, to carry that equipment when you venture into avalanche country, and to be practiced in its use.

A lightweight shovel is an essential piece of backcountry equipment. Ski poles that thread together to form a long probe are useful to probe for a buried victim. Once located, the victim hopefully can be dug out alive. Also recommended is an electronic avalanche beacon, which should be carried by each member of a backcountry party. Beacons are set on a "send" or transmit mode, emitting a signal that is audible through other beacons set on "receive" mode. If a traveler wearing a beacon set on "send" is buried in an avalanche, other members of the party can then turn their beacons to "receive" and find the victim, hopefully in time to save a life.

Better than rescuing a victim, of course, is to avoid the avalanche in the first place. Avalanche and weather information is available at the Old Faithful and Mammoth Hot Springs Hotel Bear Dens, and at the park visitor centers and ranger stations. Park personnel can inform you of general levels of avalanche danger, as well as specific areas to avoid or be aware of. You can also read the many books on snow and avalanches and use them to increase your own avalanche awareness. Two good, basic books are *A Field Guide to Snow Crystals* by Edward R. LaChapelle and *The Avalanche Book* by Betsy Armstrong and Knox Williams.

Learning about local avalanche conditions and making predictions about avalanche probabilities on your own usually involve digging pits in the snowpack and looking for signs of weakness in the various snow layers. Digging a pit in a safe location, on a slope of similar elevation and aspect as the one that concerns you, is not particularly arduous and it can be educational and fun, especially if you learn from a knowledgeable person and/or some good field guides. The various layers of snow give you a look at the history of the winter—a layer of pine needles in the snow probably indicates a period of wind, for example—and will increase your understanding and appreciation of snow and winter weather.

SKI RENTAL BUSINESSES

MAMMOTH HOT SPRINGS/GARDINER, MONTANA, AREA

PARK'S FLY SHOP
Gardiner, MT 59030
406-848-7314

TW RECREATIONAL SERVICES
THE BEAR DEN
MAMMOTH HOT SPRINGS HOTEL
Yellowstone N.P., WY 82190
307-344-7901

WEST YELLOWSTONE, MONTANA

BUD LILLY'S
39 Madison Avenue
West Yellowstone, MT 59758
406-646-7801

MADISON RIVER OUTFITTERS
125 Canyon
West Yellowstone, MT 59758
406-646-9644

YELLOWSTONE BICYCLES
132 Madison Avenue
West Yellowstone, MT 59758
406-646-7815

JACKSON, WYOMING

FLAGG RANCH RESORT
Moran, WY 83013
1-800-443-2311/
307-733-8761/
733-1572/
543-2861

JACKSON HOLE SKI AND SPORTS
485 Broadway
Jackson, WY 83001
307-733-4449

LEISURE SPORTS
974 West Broadway
Jackson, WY 83001
307-733-3040

TETON VILLAGE SPORTS
CRYSTAL SPRINGS INN
Teton Village, WY 83025
307-733-2181

WILDERNEST SPORTS
3275 West McCollister Drive
Teton Village, WY 83025
307-733-4297

OLD FAITHFUL AREA

TW RECREATIONAL SERVICES
THE BEAR DEN
OLD FAITHFUL SNOW LODGE
Yellowstone N.P., WY 82190
307-344-7901

EAST ENTRANCE/NORTH FORK OF THE SHOSHONE RIVER AREA

ABSAROKA MOUNTAIN LODGE
1231 Yellowstone Highway
Wapiti, WY 82450
307-587-3963

PAHASKA TEEPEE RESORT
183 Yellowstone Highway
Cody, WY 82414
307-527-7701

SHOSHONE LODGE
Box 790, Yellowstone Highway
Cody, WY 82414
307-587-4044

CROSS COUNTRY
SKIERS ON THE
TRAIL TO KEPLER
CASCADES, OLD
FAITHFUL

SOURCES OF INFORMATION ON WINTER TRAVEL

CODY CHAMBER OF COMMERCE
836 Sheridan Avenue
P.O. Box 2777
Cody, WY 82414
307-587-2297

FLAGG RANCH RESORT
Moran, WY 83013
1-800-433-2311/307-733-8761
543-2861/733-1572

GRAND TETON NATIONAL PARK
National Park Service
Visitor Services Office
Moran, WY 83012
307-733-2880

JACKSON CHAMBER OF
COMMERCE
532 North Cache
Jackson, WY 83001
307-733-3316

NATIONAL PARK SERVICE
Visitor Services Office
Yellowstone N.P., WY 82190
307-344-7381

PAHASKA TEEPEE RESORT
P.O. Box 2370-B
Cody, WY 82414
307-527-7701

TW RECREATIONAL SERVICES
MAMMOTH HOT SPRINGS
Yellowstone N.P., WY 82190
307-344-7901 or 344-7311
(reservations)

WEST YELLOWSTONE
CHAMBER OF COMMERCE
100 Yellowstone Avenue
West Yellowstone, MT 58758
406-646-7701; motel reservations,
406-646-7832

EIGHT

Ski Trails

CANYON RIM TRAIL

This loop trail begins and ends at the Canyon warming hut. It's 4.5 miles long, involves a 200-foot elevation change, and is considered an easy to intermediate ski.

From Canyon Junction, the Canyon Rim Trail follows North Rim Drive for about three-quarters of a mile before turning left on the access road to Inspiration Point. From here, you'll ski back up the Inspiration Point access road for half a mile or so, and then turn left and ski along the rim of the Grand Canyon of the Yellowstone for about another half mile. The trail then crosses North Rim Drive and leads through a coniferous forest to the Canyon cabin area, all closed in winter. You'll also ski past some shuttered dormitories and stores and the Canyon Visitor Center (also closed in winter) before returning to your starting point.

If you're fortunate, you may see some roof shoveling in progress on one of the summer buildings. Hardy winterkeepers, as the snow shovelers are called in Yellowstone, are responsible for relieving the buildings of their snowloads. Yellowstone lore includes many stories of buildings that suffered structural damage or collapsed altogether under the weight of accumulated snow. Recent winters in the northern Rockies have been dry, but in the past, at least, winterkeepers amassed enormous piles of snow under the eaves of buildings they cleared with simple hand tools, usually just a crosscut saw for cutting the snowpack into cubes and a shovel for skidding the heavy blocks off the roof.

On the Canyon Rim Trail you're not likely to see much large wildlife—perhaps just an old bull bison or two. You will enjoy fantastic views of the Grand Canyon of the Yellowstone River. The canyon was formed by the Yellowstone River cutting through rock that had been softened by geothermal activity. The canyon is truly an awesome spectacle, and was one of the principal reasons Yellowstone National Park was created "for the benefit and enjoyment of the people" in 1872.

Be careful along the edge of the canyon on this trail. In places, you'll have a long way to fall if you slip off the trail and over the rim of the canyon.

THE ROLLER COASTER

This 1.8-mile loop begins and ends at the Canyon warming hut. It involves a 200-foot elevation change and is considered an intermediate to difficult ski.

From the warming hut, the trail leads along the North Rim Drive for about 100 yards before turning left on a service road. This turn should be marked. You'll ski the service road for about one-third of a mile before the trail leaves the road and enters an evergreen forest. The trail then becomes a series of ups and downs—hence, the name Roller Coaster.

You're not likely to see any large wildlife on this trip. Once the trail returns to North Rim Drive after your roller-coaster rides, you'll have a choice of turning right and going directly back to Canyon Junction or of turning left and assuming the route of the Canyon Rim Trail. Skiing directly back to Canyon Junction from this point is about a half mile; the Canyon Rim Trail is described above.

WASHBURN HILLS

Skiing these mountains is recommended only for advanced skiers in good physical condition. It's also advisable that you not ski here alone and that you go into the mountains with appropriate equipment, such as avalanche transmitters, probes, shovels, and the like. Climbing skins are useful for ascending the slopes, too.

The best way to get to the great ski slopes in the Washburn Range is to travel up the road to Washburn Hot Springs Overlook and Dunraven Pass. This road is open for snow vehicles only as far as the Washburn Hot Springs Overlook, 2.5 miles north of Canyon Junction. Still, that 2.5 miles gains you about 300 vertical feet over Canyon Junction.

In winter, transportation to and around the Canyon area can be a problem. If you and your companions have your own snowmobiles, you can use them to gain access to the Washburns. If you don't have your own snow machines, you can travel to the area on rental machines or arrange with Amfac Parks and Resorts to ride a snowcoach from either Old Faithful Snow Lodge or Mammoth Hot Springs Hotel for a daylong ski tour of the Canyon area. You can choose to spend part or all of this tour skiing in the Washburns. The excursion includes a ski guide and a box lunch from Amfac, as well as having the snowcoach and driver available all day for dropoffs and pickups. You can obtain information about this service from the Bear Den Ski Shop at either Old Faithful Snow Lodge or Mammoth Hot Springs Hotel.

From the Washburn Hot Springs Overlook, you're free to climb any of the steep slopes above you. Be advised, however, that at times during some winters, the avalanche danger in these mountains is great. Before skiing in the Washburn Range, you should check with a ranger for information on snow and avalanche conditions. During the day, you usually can find a ranger on duty at the Canyon warming hut at Canyon Junction.

Views from the Washburn Hot Springs Overlook and from the slopes above can be breathtaking if the weather is clear. The long chain of mountains to the east is the Absaroka Range; it approximates the east boundary of Yellowstone National Park. To the south you'll be able to see Hayden Valley, the Red Mountains, and, far to the south, the Grand Tetons. Most of the huge reach of country that can be seen from here is devoid of people in the winter.

CASCADE LAKE TRAIL

The Cascade Lake Trail begins about one-third of a mile north of Canyon Junction on the road to Washburn Hot Springs Overlook and Dunraven Pass. The trail is only about 4 miles round-trip and involves a 150-foot elevation change. It's considered an easy ski.

From the snow vehicle road, the trail leads about 200 yards down a service road and then turns 90 degrees onto a wide trail that should be marked. A short distance farther will put you in Cascade Meadows, where there is a good chance you'll see a few large bull bison.

Cascade Meadows and Cascade Lake received their names from Cascade Creek, which drains the lake and flows through the meadows. The creek was named for its waterfall near the point where it empties into the Yellowstone River. The waterfall is called Crystal Falls, and is located between the Upper and Lower Falls of the Yellowstone River. You'll cross Cascade Creek twice on your way to Cascade Lake.

After travelling up Cascade Creek and skiing in and out of forests and meadows, you'll arrive at frozen Cascade Lake. From here you return to the trailhead along the same trail. If you're a good skier and are so inclined, you can climb up and ski down the hills in the Washburn Range above Cascade Lake. Be wary of avalanche danger, however. You can obtain information about snow and avalanche conditions at the Canyon warming hut before you begin your trip. There usually is a National Park Service employee with up-to-date information on duty at the Canyon warming hut now located in front of the visitor center.

GHOST TREES IN
BISCUIT BASIN

CHITTENDEN LOOP TRAIL

This trail begins at Tower Falls, 2.5 miles south of Tower Junction. The ski route from Tower Junction to Tower Falls is described in the Tower Falls Trail section of this chapter.

Most people who ski the Chittenden Loop Trail begin their trip by skiing from the Tower Falls Hamilton Store (closed in winter) through the Tower Falls Campground. By skiing the loop in that direction, you will be going uphill on the trail's steeper grades. If you are a good skier and snow conditions are good, you may want to ski this loop in the opposite direction by continuing up the Tower-Canyon road beyond the Tower Falls store. That way you'll be descending when you come to the steeper sections.

From the Tower Falls store this trail parallels Tower Creek for a short distance to the Tower Falls Campground. You may see some large bull elk along the Tower Creek bottom. The trail then winds through the campground before ascending an old service road. This ascent is the steepest part of the loop.

The trail continues on the service road for about 2 miles. Most of the way you'll be skiing through lodgepole pine forest, much of which burned in 1988. Depending on snow depths, you probably won't see much wildlife along this stretch of trail—perhaps just a few elk.

Your trail will bring you back to Grand Loop Road (the Tower-Canyon road) about 3 miles south of Tower Junction. If the weather is clear, you'll have a good view of Mount Washburn from this point. You

may notice the lookout and communications station on Mount Washburn. The lookout is used in summer but not in winter.

As you ski down Grand Loop Road on your way back toward Tower, you'll be paralleling the drainage of Antelope Creek; it will be on the right side of the road. You might see a few elk and bison down there. In summer, Antelope Creek is some of the best grizzly bear habitat in the Yellowstone area. Turnouts along the road you're skiing offer excellent vantages for spotting grizzlies in summer, but the Antelope Creek country itself is closed to human entry from early spring to late autumn. The summer closure has been in effect since 1983 so that this rich habitat will be free from human disturbance.

Three miles of skiing the road will bring you back to Tower Falls, and 2.5 more miles will put you at Tower Junction. From the junction, the Chittenden Loop Trail is about a 10.5-mile round-trip involving approximately 1,100 feet of elevation change. It's considered an intermediate ski.

LOST LAKE TRAIL

The Lost Lake Trail begins 1.4 miles west of Tower Junction, leads past Lost Lake to Calcite Springs, and goes from there via Grand Loop Road back to Tower Junction. It's a 4-mile trail with a 120-foot elevation change and is considered an intermediate trail. The trail is open for travel in either direction but is described here for skiing from west to east.

From the trailhead, the trail leads up the Petrified Tree access road (closed to vehicles in winter). Just one of thousands of petrified trees in the Yellowstone area, this is the only one accessible by automobile. The stone tree will be on your left, inside an iron fence, when you reach the end of the access road. A nearby tree was left outside the fence in the park's early days; that tree has been completely chiseled away by souvenir hunters.

Above Petrified Tree the trail climbs steeply for a short way and then leads through a narrow valley to Lost Lake. This is one of three Lost Lakes in Yellowstone National Park, the others being near Mammoth Hot Springs and West Thumb, respectively. You'll ski over the ice on this Lost Lake for a stretch.

A short distance beyond Lost Lake you'll come to Lost Creek. There's a short, steep descent to the bridge over Lost Creek and, depending on snow conditions, it probably would be best to remove your skis and walk down this grade.

Beyond Lost Creek you'll ski over rolling terrain, generally climbing up to the Calcite Springs Overlook on the Tower-Canyon road. From the overlook, it's about 1.5 miles back to the trailhead at Tower Junction. Sightings of elk, bison, coyotes, and other wildlife are possible all along this ski.

Skier shuttles from Mammoth are available at both ends of this trail, as they are at all the major trailheads in the Tower area. You can obtain information about coordinating your trips with the shuttle from the Bear Den Ski Shop at Mammoth Hot Springs Hotel.

TOWER FALLS TRAIL

The Tower Falls Trail begins at a large parking lot at Tower Junction. The trailhead, accessible by wheeled vehicle, is about 18 miles east of Mammoth. A skier shuttle from Mammoth Hot Springs Hotel to Tower Junction is available.

The area around Tower Junction is winter home for a number of large bull elk. You may also see some bison hereabouts, most likely bulls, but possibly some cow/calf groups as well. The bull elk will most likely be in the valley in front of the Tower Ranger Station, northwest of the road junction. The bull bison are usually to the east of the parking lot, in or around some tepid springs you'll probably notice as you ski by.

About 1.5 miles from Tower Junction you'll come to the Calcite Springs Overlook. You'll be able to see and probably smell Calcite Springs below you. The Yellowstone River is below, too, flowing through the lower end of its Grand Canyon. The jagged peak you can see to the northeast is Cutoff Mountain; clouds often catch on the summit of Cutoff. You may see some bighorn sheep around Calcite Springs Overlook or on the opposite side of the canyon, around the cliffs of columnar basalt.

You may see some bighorns around the Overhanging Cliff, too, which will loom over your head as you continue on your way to Tower Falls. Just past Overhanging Cliff you'll cross Tower Creek on the highway bridge and then pass the Tower Falls Hamilton Store (closed in winter). The path to the Tower Falls Overlook begins at the store and leads downhill from there. Depending on snow conditions, it may be safer to take your skis off and walk down this path.

Tower Falls is 132 feet high and will be mostly iced over in winter. Its name comes from the numerous towers and spires in the vicinity. Return to the Tower Junction parking lot via your outbound route to complete this 5-mile round-trip.

BLACKTAIL PLATEAU TRAIL

The Blacktail Plateau Trail follows what in the summer is known as Blacktail Plateau Drive. The road is closed to all vehicles in winter and in total is an 8-mile trail that can be skied in either direction. This is considered an intermediate trail.

The west end of the trail begins 7.5 miles east of Mammoth. A skier shuttle from the Mammoth Hot Springs Hotel is available; otherwise, you can drive your own vehicle to the trailhead.

From the west end parking lot, the trail climbs 900 vertical feet through meadows and aspen groves to a spot called the Cut; as its name implies, the Cut is a narrow notch. Your trail passes through the notch. From the Cut, the trail descends on moderate grades for about 2 miles through coniferous forest, much of it burned, until you arrive at the east end trailhead. This is on the Tower-Mammoth road about 1.4 miles west of Tower Junction.

Along the way you may see elk and bison, and possibly some mule deer and coyotes, too. You'll have great views of the country to the north, on the other side of the Yellowstone River, where the horizon line approximates the boundary between Yellowstone National Park and the Absaroka-Beartooth Wilderness Area in the Gallatin National Forest.

The high country you will be able to see to the south is part of the Washburn Mountain Range, which is in the central part of Yellowstone National Park. These mountains are great grizzly bear habitat, and undoubtedly some grizzlies will be hibernating in the Washburns while you're skiing on Blacktail Plateau.

You may arrange with the Mammoth ski shuttle to be picked up at the opposite end of the Blacktail Plateau Trail from where you begin your ski. Check at the Mammoth Hot Springs Hotel Bear Den for dropoff schedules and arrangements.

SNOW PASS TRAIL

This trail begins on the west side of Grand Loop Road about a quarter mile south of the Amfac's snowmobile rental hut near the Upper Terrace parking area. There also is a short spur trail leading from the Upper Terrace Loop Trail to the beginning of the Snow Pass Trail (see the map of Mammoth area ski trails).

From the trailhead, this trail climbs approximately 700 feet in 1.5 miles to the summit of Snow Pass. For most of that distance you'll be skiing an old wagon road. In the 1870s and early 1880s, this was the main road south from Mammoth Hot Springs into the interior of Yellowstone National Park. Because of steep grades on the way up to Snow Pass, and because snowbanks sometimes lingered there until midsummer, the road was rerouted to its present course along Glen Creek and through Kingman Pass in the 1880s.

Snow Pass is a notch between Terrace Mountain on the east and Clagett Butte on the west. Terrace Mountain got its name because the rocks there were hydrothermally formed. Even the untrained eye can see that the formations on Terrace Mountain are identical to the terraces at Mammoth Hot Springs; at one time, hot springs flowed over and created these terraces, just as limestone-charged hot water presently is building new formations at Mammoth.

From the pass, your trail descends about half a mile to the northern edge of Swan Lake Flat. There you will come to a trail junction near Upper Glen Creek. To continue your loop, turn left and ski the old road along Glen Creek for about 2.2 miles. This 2.2-mile stretch is mostly flat, and you'll probably see bull elk and possibly some bull bison along your way. Depending on snow depths, the animals most likely will be on the south-facing slopes above you, on the left side of the trail.

Once you reach Grand Loop Road (here the Mammoth-Norris road), you'll have a choice of skiing down the road to the Upper Terrace parking lot or of waiting for a pickup from the Amfac Parks and Resorts snowcoach shuttle. If you opt for the latter, check the shuttle's schedule at the activities desk at Mammoth Hot Springs Hotel before

CROSS COUNTRY SKIERS ON THE FOUNTAIN PAINT POTS TRAIL, LOWER GEYSER BASIN

you begin your ski trip. The shuttle makes regularly scheduled runs, but you must make reservations for the service in advance.

If you choose to ski down the road through Kingman Pass and past Rustic Falls on your way back to where you began your ski, be advised that you will encounter some patches of bare and wood chip–covered pavement where you will have to remove your skis and walk. Strong winds are so consistent through Kingman Pass and at some other sectors along this road that the pavement blows free of snow even in very cold and snowy winters. The wood chips are distributed on wind-scoured spots by the National Park Service to provide an operating surface for oversnow vehicles. Snowmobiles and snowcoaches negotiate the wood chips quite well; skis do not. It's about 3 miles from where you connect with the Mammoth-Norris road back to the trailhead where you started your ski.

It's 4.2 miles from the beginning of the Snow Pass Trail as described here to your junction with the Mammoth-Norris road. In

total there is a 700-foot elevation change, and the trail is considered
intermediate to difficult. The trail is open for travel in both directions,
and if you're a good skier and snow conditions are good, you may
choose to do the trail in the reverse of the way it's described here. That
way you'll be going downhill on the steep grades north of Snow Pass.

UPPER TERRACE LOOP TRAIL

This trail follows what in summer is Upper Terrace Drive. In winter, it's closed to all vehicles but open to skiing in either direction. The
trail is easiest if skied in a clockwise direction, or to your left as you
begin the ski. If skied clockwise, this is considered an easy ski; coun-
terclockwise, it's intermediate. This short trail is 1.5 miles with about
200 vertical feet of elevation change.

Along the way you'll see hot springs, as well as active and dormant
limestone terraces, and you'll have intermittent views of distant mountains through the trees. Most of the trees along the Upper Terrace Loop
are Douglas firs, but if you look closely you'll be able to spot some lim-
ber pines on the rocky outcrops along the trail. You also may see some
elk and mule deer, although those animals don't seem to be as common around the Upper Terraces as they were before the 1980s, when
there was a marked increase in human activity in the area.

Depending on the severity of the winter, you may encounter some
stretches of bare pavement along the Upper Terrace Loop. These bare
spots are caused by a combination of wind scouring and geothermal
heating. Generally, it's better to take your skis off and walk across such
places. Gouged skis are often the result if you don't.

Completing this loop will bring you back to the Upper Terrace
parking area.

INDIAN CREEK LOOP

The Indian Creek Loop is a short ski of intermediate difficulty that
begins with a snowcoach dropoff at the entrance to Indian Creek
Campground (closed in winter). The loop is about 2 miles long and
involves a 120-foot vertical elevation change.

The trail begins at your dropoff point on the Mammoth-Norris road
and leads along the campground access road past the Indian Creek
skiers' hut. The hut is an old log frame cabin that was moved to Indian
Creek from Fishing Bridge. The trail continues through the campground to the Bighorn Pass trailhead, on the west side of the campground. You'll follow the Bighorn Pass Trail for about a half mile
before the Indian Creek Loop branches off to the left. For about three-
quarters of a mile the trail follows a power line. Then it drops down to

Obsidian Creek, which it follows on the way back to the skiers' hut.

Several streams come together in this vicinity, and the area was favored trapping country for the beaver hunters of the early nineteenth century. The Gardner River and Gardner's Hole, names of two nearby features, were named for Johnson Gardner, a mountain man of the 1820s and 1830s who particularly enjoyed this locale.

Indian Creek was so named because a segment of the famous Bannock Indian Trail paralleled the stream. The Bannock Trail led from what is now Idaho to the Great Plains east of the Rocky Mountains. After about 1840, Indians from west of the Continental Divide had to travel to the Great Plains to hunt buffalo. Before 1840, tribes such as the Bannocks and the Nez Perce hunted sizable herds of buffalo along the Snake River plain on the west side of the divide. Because those herds had largely disappeared by 1840, the western tribes then had to go east to find bison. Indians used the Bannock Trail until the early 1880s, when the days of wild buffalo and free-ranging Indians came to an end.

You probably won't see much large wildlife along the Indian Creek Loop. The trail ranges in elevation from about 7,300 feet to 7,420 feet, which is a little high for most of Yellowstone's ungulates to winter over.

BIGHORN LOOP

This trail begins at the same point and for the first mile or so follows the same route as the Indian Creek Loop. It then continues to the west for another mile beyond the Indian Creek Loop and forms a loop of its own before returning to the trailhead via your outbound trail. The Bighorn Loop is a total of 5.5 miles with a 320-foot elevation change. It's considered an intermediate trail.

You'll have great views of Gardners Hole and the Gallatin Mountains on this ski. Bighorn Pass, to the west of you, is nearly 10,000 feet high. The peaks that surround Bighorn Pass are mostly over 10,000 feet. Quadrant, Antler, Holmes, and Trilobite are the names of some of the peaks in this part of the Gallatin Range. To sort them out, you can either acquire a topographic map of the area before you go on your trip or ask your snowcoach shuttle driver to stop on Swan Lake Flat at the interpretive plaque that outlines the Gallatin Range and gives the names of the peaks visible from that point. An experienced coach driver might even be able to give you the names of the various peaks from memory.

As with the Indian Creek Loop, you probably won't see much, if any, large wildlife on this trip. As an alternative, you might look for the tracks of smaller animals that do live in this high, snowy habitat. Snowshoe hares and pine martens are two common animals that can survive in this wintry world, and perhaps you'll see where their tracks cross your trail.

You'll have to arrange for your dropoff and pickup with the Mammoth ski shuttle before you go on this trip. You can make arrangements at the activities desk in the lobby of Mammoth Hot Springs Hotel.

BUNSEN PEAK TRAIL

The Bunsen Peak Trail begins on the Mammoth-Norris road about 4 miles south of Mammoth Hot Springs and follows what in summer is Bunsen Peak Road, now primarily a bicycling trail. This is a six-mile ski with a 1,120-foot elevation change. The 1,120-foot elevation change actually will be a descent as you ski back to Mammoth. Depending on snow conditions, this is an intermediate to difficult ski.

As its name suggests, the Bunsen Peak Trail circumscribes Bunsen Peak, an 8,564-foot mountain due south of Mammoth Hot Springs. It was named for Robert Wilhelm Eberhard von Bunsen, a nineteenth-century German physicist for whom the Bunsen burner also was named. You may notice a cluster of antennas and other hardware on the summit of Bunsen Peak, which make up a communications station for Yellowstone National Park.

The trail begins at the northern end of Swan Lake Flat, just upstream on Glen Creek from Rustic Falls. A snowcoach shuttle from Mammoth Hot Springs Hotel can drop you off at that point. To the west, behind you as you start your ski, are the Gallatin Mountains. The large, relatively flat-topped peak that will be closest to you is Quadrant Mountain at 10,216 feet.

From the trailhead, the Bunsen Peak Trail leads through intermittent forests and meadows for about 3 miles. Most of this stretch is fairly flat, and much of the forest burned in 1988. After skiing by some aspen groves you'll come to the beginning of a steep descent, which will continue for about 2.5 miles and amount to a 960-foot elevation loss. There are some fairly sharp curves on this downhill grade, and some stretches of trail are close to precipitous dropoffs; skiing here can be treacherous if the trail is hardpacked or icy. Sheepeater Canyon will be the steep declivity on your right as you make your descent. The Gardner River flows at the bottom of the canyon.

The trail continues winding down and around Bunsen Peak until you make a bridge crossing of Glen Creek—the same Glen Creek you crossed at the beginning of your ski. The creek flows around the west side of the mountain while you ski around the east. Shortly beyond Glen Creek, you'll enter a National Park Service utility and residential area, where the ski trail ends and a plowed road commences. At this point you'll probably have to remove your skis and walk through the housing area to the Mammoth-Norris road, only about a quarter mile away. An Amfac Parks and Resorts shuttle van will pick you up at the junction of the housing area access road and the Mammoth-Norris road. If you don't feel like waiting, you may walk back to Mammoth Hot Springs Hotel. The hotel is less than a mile down the road from the junction.

Sightings of elk, coyotes, mule deer, and bison are possible on this trip. You can obtain information about shuttles for this and other ski trips in the Mammoth area at either the Bear Den Ski Shop or the activities desk at Mammoth Hot Springs Hotel.

SHEEPEATER TRAIL

This trail begins with a snowcoach dropoff at the entrance to Indian Creek Campground (closed in winter). From there, the trail parallels Grand Loop Road for about a half mile to the side road to Sheepeater Cliff. This road is closed to all vehicles in winter, so skiers have it to themselves.

After leaving Grand Loop Road, you'll ski a short distance to Sheepeater Cliff, a basaltic formation named for the Sheepeater Indians. The Sheepeaters were a branch of the Shoshone tribe and were so named because bighorn sheep comprised a large portion of their diet. The Sheepeaters were the only group of Indians living more or less year-round in what is now Yellowstone National Park at the time of Anglo discovery and exploration.

From Sheepeater Cliff, the trail leads along the east side of Swan Lake Flat. Good views of the Gallatin Mountain Range to the west and the Gardner River Canyon (also known as Sheepeater Canyon) to the east are possible if the weather is clear. Much of the forest in this area burned in 1988.

Depending on snow depths, you should be able to spot some bull elk and bull bison somewhere on or around Swan Lake Flat. Windswept and/or south-facing slopes around the flat are the most likely places for bison, especially if the snow is deep.

After skirting the edge of Swan Lake Flat for about 2.5 miles, the Sheepeater Trail connects with the Bunsen Peak Trail. Turning left on the latter will take you about 1.6 miles back to Grand Loop Road, where with prior arrangements the Amfac Parks and Resorts skier shuttle can pick you up and return you to Mammoth Hot Springs Hotel.

The Sheepeater Trail is 5 miles with only a 60-foot elevation change. It's flat, easy going, and is considered an easy ski.

FAIRY FALLS TRAIL

A ski trip to Fairy Falls begins with a snowcoach dropoff at the trailhead on Fountain Flats Drive. Information about schedules and charges for snowcoach dropoffs can be obtained from the Old Faithful Snow Lodge Bear Den.

From the Fairy Falls trailhead it's about 1.3 miles to a fork in the trail. Skiing a short distance on the right fork will take you to Fairy Meadow, which you might want to do as a side trip. Look for bison out in the meadow and for elk along the fringes of timber. You may see or hear coyotes here, too. The rounded hills you'll notice at the upper end of the meadow are the Twin Buttes. They are heavily influenced by geo-thermal activity.

Taking the left fork at the trail junction will continue you on your way to Fairy Falls, which will appear after another mile or so as an ice column on the side of a cliff. The cliff is the edge of the Madison Plateau.

From the falls back to Old Faithful is about 8.5 miles. Your return route will take you back to the Fairy Falls trailhead and from there along the snow vehicle road to Biscuit Basin. Your route from Biscuit Basin to Old Faithful is described in the Biscuit Basin Loop Trail section of this chapter.

Another route back to Old Faithful from Fairy Falls will take you past Imperial Geyser and over the plateau country between the geyser and Biscuit Basin. This is a long, difficult ski over a trail that is rarely used and may not even be broken. The trip is not recommended for anyone other than an excellent skier in excellent condition, and then not without a headlamp and at least a minimum of survival gear. At least once a winter, it seems, a party will attempt to ski over the Plateau Trail from Fairy Falls and get caught out overnight. Twice while working for the National Park Service at Old Faithful, the author spent an entire night out looking for overdue skiers who tried to do the Plateau Trail and ran out of daylight. Fortunately, neither of those incidents resulted in anything more serious than cold, tired skiers (as well as cold, tired searchers).

The Fairy Falls trip by the recommended route is about 11 miles with approximately 160 feet of elevation change. By the recommended route, this is considered an easy ski.

PARK VISITORS
SKIING TOWARD
UPPER GEYSER
BASIN

MYSTIC FALLS TRAIL

The Mystic Falls Trail begins at the Old Faithful Snow Lodge, crosses the snow vehicle parking lot to the Old Faithful Visitor Center, and from there leads past the front of the Old Faithful Inn. Follow the signs from

there to Biscuit Basin, a route that is described in the Biscuit Basin
Loop Trail section of this chapter.

In Biscuit Basin, follow the boardwalk from the parking area over
the Firehole River bridge and through the various hot springs. Because
some stretches of boardwalk may be bare of snow and still others may
be icy from accumulations of frozen spray and steam, you may find it
easier to walk rather than ski through Biscuit Basin.

At the far side of the thermal area you will find the beginning of the
trail to Mystic Falls; it should be marked. A short distance (50 yards or
so) from the trailhead, you'll come to a junction. Taking the left fork
will put you on the Summit Lake Trail—a very arduous ski—whereas
the right fork will continue you on your way toward Mystic Falls. This
route basically parallels the Little Firehole River for about a mile until
you arrive at Mystic Falls. The trail from Biscuit Basin to Mystic Falls is
moderately uphill through coniferous forest. There is some sidehilling,

too, where in some years there is a degree of avalanche danger. The route also takes you through some isolated thermal areas where you may see some cow elk. Most of the forest in this area burned very hot on September 7, 1988; the North Fork Fire passed through here on its way to Old Faithful, where later that day it developed into a full-scale firestorm.

From Mystic Falls, return to Biscuit Basin via your outbound trail. In Biscuit Basin you'll have the option of continuing back toward Old Faithful on your outbound trail or taking an alternate trail that turns to your right at the edge of Biscuit Basin and leads over a bridge on the Little Firehole River. This trail then leads across Grand Loop Road, along the southern fringe of the Biscuit Basin thermal area, and from there through some small meadows and patches of lodgepole timber to the neighborhood of Daisy Geyser. At Daisy you will turn left, ski downhill a couple of hundred yards, and rejoin your outbound trail in the Upper Geyser Basin. From that point it's less than a mile back to Old Faithful. There is no appreciable difference in distance between these

two return routes, but in a dry or mild winter the alternate trail from Biscuit Basin over the Little Firehole River probably will offer better snow conditions. That's because it passes through country that is somewhat less influenced by geothermal activity.

Round-trip from Old Faithful, the Mystic Falls Trail is about 7 miles, with no significant elevation change between Old Faithful and Biscuit Basin. Between Biscuit Basin and Mystic Falls there is an elevation change of about 80 vertical feet, and overall this trip is considered an easy to intermediate ski. You will see wildlife along the way, certainly elk and bison and possibly mule deer, coyotes, waterfowl, and eagles. Look for the eagles in the trees around the Biscuit Basin thermal area. As always, if you give the wildlife their space, they'll give you yours.

BULL ELK IN
BISCUIT BASIN

BISCUIT BASIN LOOP TRAIL

This route begins at the Old Faithful Snow Lodge, crosses the snowcoach and snowmobile parking lot to the Old Faithful Visitor Center, and then continues down the trail through the Upper Geyser Basin. Your route will take you past Old Faithful Geyser, the Old Faithful Inn, and Castle Geyser.

About 1 mile from Snow Lodge the trail will pass Grotto Geyser on your right. The unusual arches and windows in Grotto's cone were created when dissolved silica in discharged water accreted on tree trunks around the geyser's vent.

Just beyond Grotto is Riverside Geyser. There's a short half-moon path off the main trail that leads to a good view of Riverside. The next expected eruption time for Riverside may be posted on a sign at this point. As its name suggests, Riverside is situated on the bank of the Firehole River, and when it erupts it sends a plume of water and steam angling out over the stream. From the right vantage point and with the right lighting conditions, you can see a lovely rainbow that forms an arc over the river in the geyser mist.

Just beyond Riverside your trail will take you over the Firehole on an old roadway bridge. Immediately over the bridge on your left will be Fan and Mortar Geysers, and just beyond them will be Morning Glory Pool. Morning Glory is a beautiful pool that got its name from its resemblance to the flower of the same name. Unfortunately, vandalism has greatly altered the appearance of the pool since its naming. The scalloped rim of sinter that originally ringed the pool was long ago broken off and hauled away by souvenir hunters, and so many objects have been thrown into the pool by passersby that the throat of the spring has been partially clogged. With its hot water inflow thus inhibited, the pool has cooled to the point that bacteria and algae are now able to grow where originally they could not. The presence of these living organisms has paled the pool's former azure color.

The area around Riverside and Morning Glory and from there down to Biscuit Basin is winter range for a number of large bull elk. They often offer great photographic possibilities, especially if they can be framed with one of the area's many thermal features.

Between Morning Glory Pool and Biscuit Basin the trail passes through lodgepole pine timber on an old roadcut. Some of the timber burned in 1988. Just after you top the rise on the old roadway, you'll pass Artemesia and Atomizer Geysers. They'll be on your left under a stone retaining wall.

A short distance farther will put you in Biscuit Basin proper. Named for peculiar biscuit-shaped dollops of sinter that originally were formed by some of the hot springs here, Biscuit Basin is winter home for numerous elk and bison. You may see a few mule deer here, too, as well as some waterfowl along the river. Crossing Grand Loop Road will put you on a boardwalk leading past most of the major springs in Biscuit Basin. Depending on snow and ice conditions, it may be better to remove your skis and walk the boardwalk.

From the Biscuit Basin boardwalk you have a choice of returning to Old Faithful the way you came or skiing a short distance up the Mystic Falls Trail and turning left on a trail that bridges the Little Firehole River and then crosses Grand Loop Road a few hundred yards south of where you crossed it earlier. This trail then leads through a mile-or-so stretch of small meadows and lodgepole timber to Daisy Geyser, where it turns left and rejoins the Upper Geyser Basin Trail you skied as you were leaving Old Faithful. From the point where you rejoin the Upper Geyser Basin Trail it's about 1 mile back to Old Faithful. In total, this loop is about 5 miles with no significant elevation change.

BLACK SAND BASIN TRAIL

Begin this ski at the Bear Den and from there ski across the Snow Lodge parking lot to the Old Faithful Visitor Center. From the visitor center follow the signs toward Morning Glory Pool.

This route will take you in front of the Old Faithful Inn (closed in winter), which was built during the winter of 1903–1904. You might want to pause for a moment and consider the difficulties that must have been involved in constructing such a building in winter in the days before snowcoaches or snowmobiles or modern building equipment. The author spent a lot of time in such contemplation in the winter of 1980–1981, when a large crew of men took the entire winter just to reroof the grand old building. Only the old house of the inn was built that first winter. The east wing, or the wing closer to Old Faithful Geyser, was added in 1913; the west wing was built in 1927.

From Old Faithful Inn the trail continues past Castle Geyser, where a sign predicting the geyser's next eruption should be posted. You'll notice that Castle has an exceptionally large sinter cone. Geologists have determined that silica from the geyser's mineral-laden water accreted on the trunks of trees that grew at the site before Castle became active. The tree trunks thus became the structural framework for Castle's formation. Of course, it's not hard to guess how Castle Geyser got its name: Members of the Washburn Expedition, a government exploration party that first came through Yellowstone in 1870, thought the geyser resembled "an old feudal tower partially in ruins."

You may encounter some snow-free pavement by Castle Geyser. Actually, the trail to Black Sand Basin passes over a number of "hot spots" that are apt to be bare. It's best to take your skis off and walk over these spots—gravel will probably put some deep gouges in your ski bottoms if you don't.

You'll almost certainly see wildlife on this ski, too. The large flat between Old Faithful Geyser and Castle Geyser is a good place to see bison and elk as well as Canada geese. If you're out early in the morning, before other people are out in numbers, you may see a coyote or two or at least hear them howling.

From Castle Geyser the trail continues on a parallel with the Firehole River; the river winds over quite close to the trail for a stretch. The trail you are skiing follows what used to be a segment of Grand Loop Road. The National Park Service rerouted this stretch of road in the early 1970s to remove auto traffic from the Upper Geyser Basin.

About 1 mile from Snow Lodge you'll come to a trail junction where turning left will take you past Daisy Geyser. A short ski through some meadows and lodgepole pines will bring you to present-day Grand Loop Road, and crossing the road will put you in the Black Sand Basin thermal area. You may want to spend some time walking or skiing (depending on snow and ice conditions) around Black Sand admiring the geothermal features there. Iron Spring Creek is the stream that flows through this area. Summer anglers consistently pull surprisingly large trout from this small stream.

From Black Sand Basin you return to Old Faithful via the same route you followed on your way out. It's a 4-mile round-trip from Snow Lodge with very minimal elevation change. This is considered an easy ski.

LONE STAR GEYSER/HOWARD EATON TRAIL LOOP

The Lone Star Geyser/Howard Eaton Trail Loop is probably the most popular ski in the Old Faithful area. The loop, open for two-way travel, amounts to a 7-mile round-trip from Old Faithful Snow Lodge. Skiing the 7-mile loop involves a 500-foot elevation change.

This trail may be considered intermediate to difficult, depending on whether one skis up or down the Howard Eaton Trail segment of the loop. There is a stretch of steep trail with some fairly sharp curves along the Howard Eaton Trail. Going uphill on that stretch is not particularly difficult, but going downhill there can be treacherous, especially if snow conditions are hardpacked or icy.

If you decide to go to Lone Star Geyser via the Lone Star Trail, you'll begin your ski at the Bear Den Ski Shop and follow the signs past the Old Faithful Lodge (closed in winter) and over a bridge on the Firehole River. Just beyond the bridge you'll come to a trail junction, where the left fork leads to Mallard Lake and the right fork will continue you on your way to Lone Star. You may see some elk or bison among the thermal features in this vicinity.

From the trail junction the Lone Star Trail leads you uphill along an old roadcut and the existing Grand Loop Road to Kepler Cascades, named for Kepler Hoyt, the young son of the governor of Wyoming. The boy visited Yellowstone National Park with his father in 1881. The cascades are worth a look, and a few ravens are almost always perched in the trees around the Kepler Cascades viewing platform. The ravens are accustomed to humans so you can probably take some good pictures of them with only an intermediate-length telephoto lens.

Beyond Kepler, the Lone Star Trail follows an old road for about 2 miles to Lone Star Geyser. You'll be paralleling the Firehole River for that distance and will cross it by bridge at one point. You may see some waterfowl along the river and possibly some bull bison on the trail or in the small geothermal alcoves through which the trail passes. The bulls shouldn't be any problem for you if you give them space.

Lone Star Geyser erupts approximately every three hours for a period of about thirty minutes. There is a sign identifying the geyser, but your eye probably would catch it anyway because of its large sinter cone.

At Lone Star Geyser you'll have a choice of returning to Old Faithful via the Lone Star road or descending the Howard Eaton Trail. Remember, going down Howard Eaton Trail involves some steep skiing, and it's not recommended unless you're a good skier and snow conditions are pretty good, too. If you do descend the Howard Eaton Trail, after a mile or so you'll ski into a burned area, still another legacy of the spectacular fires that burned in and around the Old Faithful area in September 1988. Later that autumn, a trail crew spent many days on this section of trail clearing snags that fell during and after the fires. Snags totalling several hundred per mile of trail had to be cut before skiing was possible the following winter.

The bottom of the Howard Eaton Trail will bring you back to Grand Loop Road. Following the signs will return you to the Bear Den. The whole Lone Star Loop will require a couple of hours to nearly a full day, depending on your ability and snow conditions.

MALLARD LAKE/MALLARD CREEK LOOP

The Mallard Lake Trail begins at the Snow Lodge Bear Den, leads through some other buildings and cabins in the Old Faithful area, crosses the Firehole River by bridge a short distance from the Old Faithful Lodge (closed in winter), and then begins a moderate climb through intermittently burned forest. From the Bear Den to Mallard Lake is approximately 6.6 miles round-trip and amounts to about an 800-foot elevation gain and loss.

You may see a few elk and bison around the trail crossing of the Firehole River and perhaps on your left along the lower reaches of the trail after it enters the forest above the river. For the most part, though, large wildlife are absent from this trail. You will see a lot of burned trees along your ski. They were killed by the North Fork Fire in September 1988.

On your way up the hill you'll round what local skiers call the Mae West Curve—you'll know it when you see it. It's not that big a deal when you're going uphill, but if you come back this way it will be an achievement if you can round Mae West without falling.

Above the Mae West Curve and before you reach Mallard Lake, you'll pass through a narrow notch between two rocky bluffs. Boulders are strewn about below the bluffs and along the trail. This site is typical of much of the surrounding plateau country, where abrupt and rocky breaks like the one you're skiing through are interspersed with expanses of otherwise fairly flat terrain.

Mallard Lake itself marks the focal point of what geologists call a resurgent dome, a spot where volcanic pressure inside the earth is welling up and creating a dome or bubble on the earth's surface. Looking at frozen and snow-covered Mallard Lake, it's hard to appreciate the igneous forces at work a relatively short distance below the surface. The Mallard Lake resurgent dome is one of two such features in Yellowstone National Park. The other is centered under Stonetop Mountain a few miles northeast of Yellowstone Lake.

At Mallard Lake you'll have the option of returning to Old Faithful the way you came or continuing beyond Mallard Lake down the drainage of Mallard Creek. Be advised that the Mallard Creek Trail is exceptionally steep and twisting, and is recommended only for very good skiers and for them only in good snow conditions. A friend broke a ski there and had to walk over the snow all the way back to Old Faithful—

she was tired by the time she got back, to say the least.

If you do decide to go down the Mallard Creek Trail, you will descend about 800 vertical feet to Grand Loop Road, which the trail intersects a short distance up the Firehole River from Midway Geyser Basin. At this point you're almost certain to see bison and cow elk; they're nearly always present in the dead lodgepole pines where Mallard Creek flows into the Firehole. That stand of dead trees will be on the other side of the road and slightly to your right when you reach the bottom of the trail.

From the mouth of Mallard Creek the return trail to Old Faithful leads along a power line to Biscuit Basin. You're apt to see elk and bison along the power line, and Biscuit Basin itself is an excellent place to see adult bull elk. The trail from Biscuit Basin will lead you up an old roadcut, past Artemesia and Atomizer Geysers (they'll be on your right beneath a stone retaining wall), and down to Morning Glory Pool. From Morning Glory it's 1.1 miles back to Snow Lodge on the trail through the Upper Geyser Basin. You're sure to see more wildlife, most likely elk and bison, along the way. All told, the Mallard Lake/ Mallard Creek Loop is 12 miles. The Mallard Creek segment of the loop is a very difficult trail recommended only for advanced skiers.

FERN CASCADES TRAIL

The Fern Cascades Trail is a 3-mile, one-way loop that begins and ends at the Old Faithful Snow Lodge Bear Den. From the Bear Den, follow the signs and arrows across Grand Loop Road and through the National Park Service residential area. At the edge of the residential area, the trail enters a burned forest and immediately begins a fairly steep 250-foot climb. At the top of your climb, where the topography begins to flatten out, you'll come to a trail junction. Taking the right fork of the junction will lead you one-tenth of a mile to the Fern Cascades overlook.

These cascades on a fork of Iron Spring Creek are worth a look. Returning from the cascades to the trail junction will put you back on the Fern Cascades Loop. Remember, it's a one-way trail, designated that way because of its steep and narrow nature as it ascends from the park service housing area. From the Fern Cascades junction you'll ski another 2 miles or so through rolling country before you come to a moderately steep descent. Here you'll give up the elevation you gained on your climb at the beginning of the trail. At the bottom of this run-out, the trail again crosses Grand Loop Road, so don't kamikaze down the slope and into the road without first checking for snowcoach and snowmobile traffic.

The Fern Cascades Loop is considered an intermediate trail. It's a

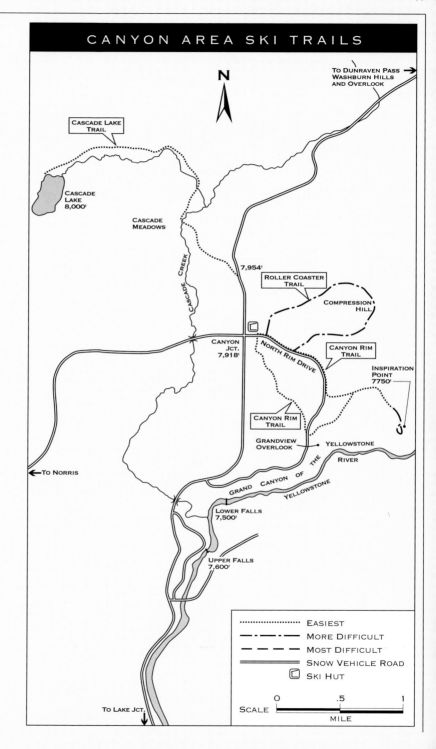

CANYON AREA SKI TRAILS

N

TO DUNRAVEN PASS
WASHBURN HILLS
AND OVERLOOK

CASCADE LAKE
TRAIL

CASCADE
LAKE
8,000'

CASCADE
MEADOWS

CASCADE CREEK

7,954'

ROLLER COASTER
TRAIL

COMPRESSION
HILL

CANYON
JCT.
7,918'

NORTH RIM DRIVE

CANYON RIM
TRAIL

INSPIRATION
POINT
7750'

CANYON RIM
TRAIL

GRANDVIEW
OVERLOOK

YELLOWSTONE
RIVER

←TO NORRIS

GRAND CANYON OF THE YELLOWSTONE

LOWER FALLS
7,500'

UPPER FALLS
7,600'

EASIEST
MORE DIFFICULT
MOST DIFFICULT
SNOW VEHICLE ROAD
SKI HUT

TO LAKE JCT.

0   .5   1
SCALE
MILE

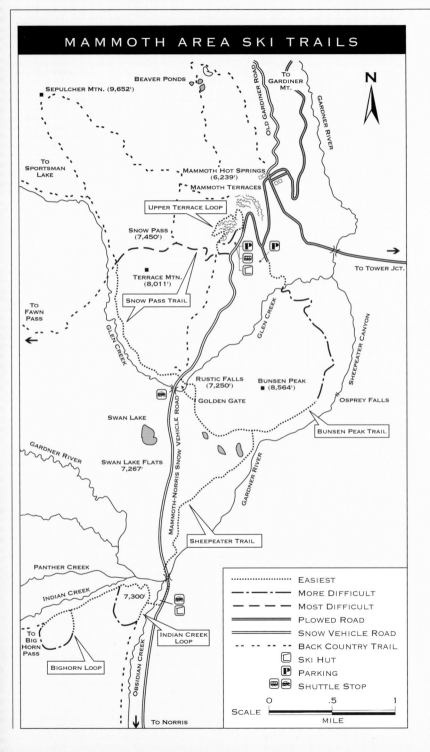

MAMMOTH AREA SKI TRAILS

BEAVER PONDS

TO GARDINER MT.

SEPULCHER MTN. (9,652')

OLD GARDINER ROAD

GARDNER RIVER

TO SPORTSMAN LAKE

MAMMOTH HOT SPRINGS (6,239')

MAMMOTH TERRACES

UPPER TERRACE LOOP

SNOW PASS (7,450')

TERRACE MTN. (8,011')

SNOW PASS TRAIL

TO FAWN PASS

GLEN CREEK

GLEN CREEK

TO TOWER JCT.

RUSTIC FALLS (7,250')

BUNSEN PEAK (8,564')

SHEEPEATER CANYON

OSPREY FALLS

GOLDEN GATE

BUNSEN PEAK TRAIL

SWAN LAKE

MAMMOTH-NORRIS SNOW VEHICLE ROAD

GARDNER RIVER

SWAN LAKE FLATS 7,267'

GARDNER RIVER

SHEEPEATER TRAIL

PANTHER CREEK

INDIAN CREEK

7,300'

TO BIG HORN PASS

INDIAN CREEK LOOP

BIGHORN LOOP

OBSIDIAN CREEK

TO NORRIS

SCALE
0   .5   1
MILE

- ···················· EASIEST
- —·—·—·— MORE DIFFICULT
- — — — — MOST DIFFICULT
- ═══════ PLOWED ROAD
- ─────── SNOW VEHICLE ROAD
- –· –· –· – BACK COUNTRY TRAIL
- 🏠 SKI HUT
- Ⓟ PARKING
- 🚐 SHUTTLE STOP

N

TOWER AREA SKI TRAILS

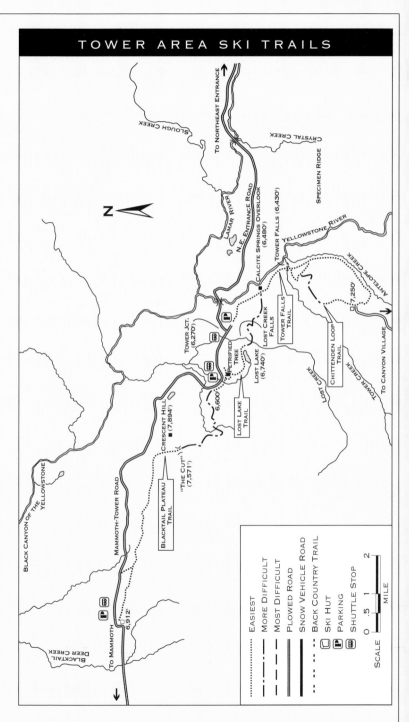

N

TO NORTHEAST ENTRANCE

SLOUGH CREEK

CRYSTAL CREEK

SPECIMEN RIDGE

LAMAR RIVER

N.E. ENTRANCE ROAD

CALCITE SPRINGS OVERLOOK (6,480')

TOWER FALLS (6,430')

YELLOWSTONE RIVER

ANTELOPE CREEK

7,250'

TO CANYON VILLAGE

TOWER JCT. (6,270')

PETRIFIED TREE

LOST LAKE (6,740')

LOST CREEK FALLS

TOWER FALLS TRAIL

CHITTENDEN LOOP TRAIL

LOST CREEK

TOWER CREEK

6,600'

LOST LAKE TRAIL

CRESCENT HILL ■ (7,894')

"THE CUT" (7,571')

BLACKTAIL PLATEAU TRAIL

BLACK CANYON OF THE YELLOWSTONE

MAMMOTH-TOWER ROAD

6,912'

BLACKTAIL DEER CREEK

TO MAMMOTH

EASIEST

MORE DIFFICULT

MOST DIFFICULT

PLOWED ROAD

SNOW VEHICLE ROAD

BACK COUNTRY TRAIL

SKI HUT   PARKING   SHUTTLE STOP

SCALE   0   .5   1   2

MILE

OLD FAITHFUL AREA SKI TRAILS

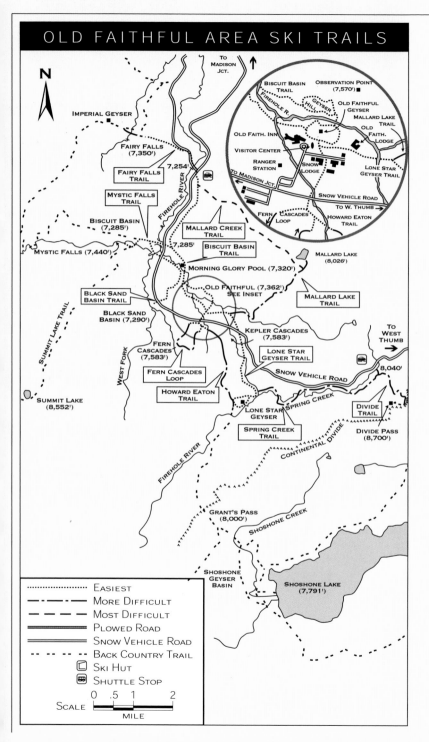

N

To
MADISON
JCT.

IMPERIAL GEYSER

BISCUIT BASIN
TRAIL

OBSERVATION POINT
(7,570') ■

FIREHOLE R.

GEYSER
HILL

OLD FAITHFUL
GEYSER

MALLARD LAKE
TRAIL

OLD
FAITH.
LODGE

OLD FAITH. INN

FAIRY FALLS
(7,350')

VISITOR CENTER

7,254'

RANGER
STATION

SNOW
LODGE

TO MADISON JCT.

LONE STAR
GEYSER TRAIL

FAIRY FALLS
TRAIL

SNOW VEHICLE ROAD

MYSTIC FALLS
TRAIL

FERN   CASCADES
LOOP

HOWARD EATON
TRAIL

TO W. THUMB

BISCUIT BASIN
(7,285')

MALLARD CREEK
TRAIL

7,285'

MALLARD LAKE
(8,026')

MYSTIC FALLS (7,440')

BISCUIT BASIN
TRAIL

MORNING GLORY POOL (7,320')

SUMMIT LAKE TRAIL

BLACK SAND
BASIN TRAIL

OLD FAITHFUL (7,362')
SEE INSET

MALLARD LAKE
TRAIL

BLACK SAND
BASIN (7,290')

KEPLER CASCADES
(7,583')

To
WEST
THUMB

WEST FORK

FERN
CASCADES
(7,583')

LONE STAR
GEYSER TRAIL

SNOW VEHICLE ROAD

8,040'

FERN CASCADES
LOOP

HOWARD EATON
TRAIL

SUMMIT LAKE
(8,552')

LONE STAR
GEYSER

SPRING CREEK

DIVIDE
TRAIL

SPRING CREEK
TRAIL

DIVIDE PASS
(8,700')

FIREHOLE RIVER

CONTINENTAL DIVIDE

GRANT'S PASS
(8,000')

SHOSHONE CREEK

SHOSHONE
GEYSER
BASIN

SHOSHONE LAKE
(7,791')

good one to do when you have only a half day or so to ski. For almost its entire length, the trail passes through blackened forest that burned spectacularly on September 7, 1988, when the North Fork Fire roared through this area. You probably won't see any large wildlife on this ski, with the possible exception being along Myriad Creek, a small stream near the Old Faithful Snow Lodge that the Fern Trail bridges a short distance from the Bear Den Ski Shop. Elk and bison sometimes feed in and along Myriad Creek.

CROSS COUNTRY SKIER SHAWN JOYCE AT FOUNTAIN PAINT POTS, LOWER GEYSER BASIN

DIVIDE LOOKOUT/SPRING CREEK TRAIL

Divide Lookout was an old fire tower that stood on the Continental Divide about 7 or 8 miles east of Old Faithful. The tower had not been used as a fire lookout for many years and recently was removed from the site. The trail leading up to the site of the old tower is still a popular ski.

Most people who ski to Divide Lookout begin their trip with a snowcoach dropoff at the trailhead. Snowcoach shuttles to trailheads in the Old Faithful area are available at intervals throughout the morning hours. Check at the Old Faithful Snow Lodge Bear Den for schedules.

From the trailhead to the site of the old tower is about 1.7 miles up moderately steep grades. The lookout is 8,779 feet high, or approximately 750 vertical feet higher than the trailhead. There is one fairly sharp, left-hand curve in the trail on your way down, but you'll notice it on your way up so you can be prepared.

Views through the trees on your way to the lookout are spectacular—remember, you'll be on or near the Continental Divide on this ski. Shoshone Lake and the Grand Teton Mountains will be in sight to the south, and Yellowstone Lake and the Absaroka Mountains will be to the

east. If you're fortunate enough to make this trip in early winter on a
calm day, you may be able to hear the sounds of ice forming on the
two lakes. Groans and cracks and other weird noises reminiscent of
whale songs emanate from the big lakes during freeze-up, and at times
the music is audible from Divide Lookout.

You may take note of the forest on your way to and
from Divide Lookout. Most of the trees you see will be
Yellowstone's ubiquitous lodgepole pines, but some
Engelmann spruce and subalpine fir and a few whitebark pines are present at this elevation, too. You can
distinguish whitebark pines from lodgepoles by their
lighter-colored, more scaly bark and by the fact that
their needles are grouped in clusters of three to five;
lodgepole needles, on the other hand, are always in
pairs.

Most years whitebark pines produce few if any
cones, but every few years the trees produce a prodigious cone crop. When that happens, grizzly bears and a
host of other animals and birds capitalize on the bo-
nanza of nutritious pine seeds. While working on a grizzly bear study project one autumn, the author noted
several spots along the Divide Lookout Trail where grizzlies had been feeding on whitebark pinecones.

Returning almost to the trailhead will bring you to a
trail junction where turning left will put you on the
Spring Creek Trail and the way back to Old Faithful
(going straight will take you back to the trailhead where
the snowcoach dropped you off). The Spring Creek Trail
is a long, gradual descent. You'll cross and recross
Spring Creek numerous times on footbridges before
intersecting the Lone Star Geyser Trail along the upper
Firehole River. From the intersection with the Lone Star Trail you'll
have about 3 more miles to return to Old Faithful. All told, skiing to
Divide Lookout and then back to Old Faithful via Spring Creek is about
an 11.5-mile trip. You're not likely to see any large animals along the
way, with the exception of possibly a bull bison or two along the Lone
Star Trail. You may also see a few elk and bison among the geothermal
features near the Mallard Lake Trail junction, which you will pass just
before you get back to the Old Faithful developed area.

WINTER VISITOR
PHOTOGRAPHING
WILDLIFE, GIBBON
CANYON, NEAR OLD
FAITHFUL

Wildlife

Winter is a bottleneck through which Yellowstone's wildlife populations are annually squeezed. Scarce food and harsh weather are the elements that eliminate summer's surplus as nature weighs its components and achieves its balance.

When Yellowstone National Park was created in 1872, its boundaries were drawn more to protect the area's geothermal basins than to protect its wildlife. The land preserved "near the head-waters of the Yellow stone river" is mostly high country; good summer range, but because of deep snow and cold temperatures largely unsuitable as winter habitat for most animals. The herds of bison, elk, bighorn sheep, and other species seen feeding on lush vegetation in central Yellowstone Park in summer must adopt different strategies to survive the area's hard winters. For most animals, this means leaving the high country and migrating either to lower elevations or to one of the park's thermal basins. The maps in this chapter locate the Yellowstone area's major wintering grounds and also give some idea of ungulate migration patterns between winter and summer ranges. The maps were furnished through the courtesy of Frank Singer, a research biologist with the National Park Service in Yellowstone National Park.

For large grazing animals, Yellowstone's winter can be seen as a long period of energy drain, a time when the meager forage an animal is able to find does not equal the expenditure of energy required to survive. The answer to the question of survival is determined by how

FROSTY BISON
CONGREGATE IN
THERMAL AREA OF
OLD FAITHFUL

successful an animal was in laying on reserves of fat during the previous summer and autumn and how successfully it conserves those reserves during the winter and early spring. Many factors enter into the survival equation, such as an individual animal's age, overall herd size, number of competing species, and, of course, severity of winter weather. An often overlooked but perhaps most important element is the condition of the summer range the previous year, which in the Yellowstone area is largely determined by moisture patterns. Moist years yield good forage production whereas dry years provide poor yields. Heavy dieoffs among herbivores often occur in winters following dry growing seasons; indeed, a heavy winterkill is more than anything else an indication that herds entered the winter in less than prime condition.

If you spend some time watching large mammals during your winter tour of Yellowstone, you'll be able to see how those animals employ conservation strategies to minimize their energy losses. Both elk and bison, for example, frequently travel single file to take advantage of the trail broken by their leader. Both species inhabit the park's thermal basins, where geothermal influence reduces snow depth and keeps some ground free of snow altogether. If you watch long enough, you will see how wildlife in the thermal areas move from basin to basin along logical corridors offering the least resistance to their passage, such as along hydrothermal runoff channels or over hardpacked snowmobile roads.

BULL ELK SEEKING FORAGE DURING A HARSH WINTER, FIREHOLE RIVER

On extremely cold nights both elk and bison gather in places where geothermal radiation is greatest and bed overnight on the warm earth. An example of these cold-weather bedding areas is the lower end of the parking lot in front of the Old Faithful Inn, near the point where the road leaves the lot and just west of the ski trail between Old Faithful Geyser and Castle Geyser. Another example is on the northeast side of Old Faithful Geyser, just west of where the trail to Geyser Hill branches off the boardwalk around Old Faithful. If you happen by one of these spots when it's not occupied by elk or bison, take off your glove and feel the earth. It will be warm to the touch, regardless of how cold the weather is. Even if animals are absent from the snow-free hot spots, as they often are at midday, you will be able to recognize the bedding areas by the large numbers of buffalo chips and elk pellets on the ground, an unmistakable sign of intensive use. You may be able to spot other warm-ground bedding areas on your own.

Geothermal activity is much less prevalent on Yellowstone's Northern Range than it is in the central part of the park. Up north, lower elevations and a milder climate are the keys to survival for large mammals. Remember, "lower elevations" and "milder climate" are relative attributes. Even the lowest valleys in northern Yellowstone are above 5,000 feet, and the climate there, though much less severe than

that on Yellowstone's high plateaus, is still harsh compared to most places in the United States.

On the Northern Range, steep, south-facing slopes form the core of the winter range and are somewhat analogous to the hot spots found in geothermal wintering grounds. Because of their steepness and compass aspect, south-facing slopes effectively enjoy a high angle of solar incidence, even in midwinter, and often remain totally or nearly snow-free even during cold snaps. Consequently, forage for grazing species is more easily obtained, and bare sunny slopes are warmer resting areas than shady, snowy sites. The extensive Hellroaring Slopes, just east of Hellroaring Creek and visible from the Hellroaring Overlook along the Mammoth-Tower road, are good examples of sunny southern exposures that offer winter habitat for grazers. Many elk and lesser numbers of bison, mule deer, and bighorn sheep utilize that particular area.

BULL BISON SKULL IN DRIFTED SNOW, FIREHOLE RIVER

On the Northern Range, in Hayden Valley, and in a few other places in Yellowstone, some wintering herbivores survive by using windswept ridge crests and hilltops. Winter winds reliably blow those high points free or relatively free of snow. Windswept ridges are usable habitat primarily for bison and bull elk, probably because the large size of these animals enables them to survive in such exposed places.

The problem common to foraging in thermal basins, south-facing slopes, and windswept ridge crests is that by nature these areas are all hot, dry places during summer, so plant growth there is rather minimal. Still, all three areas offer microclimates where animals can rest, move around more freely, and find a little food.

In addition, all three areas offer a better alternative than trying to survive elsewhere, where the general snow depth is often two to six feet on the level. Remember, too, that the key to survival seems to be how successfully an animal conserves those stores of energy accumulated during the previous summer rather than a question of how successfully it forages on the winter range. With this in mind, you can see that the opportunity to simply lie or stand still in a relatively warm, snow-free place is an important aspect of a wintering ground.

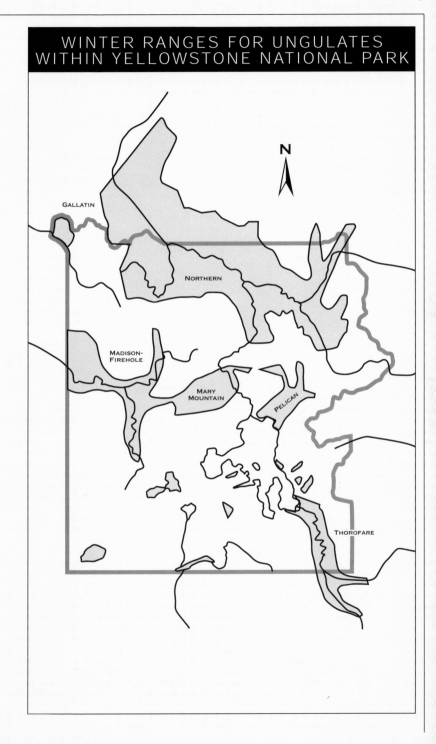

WINTER RANGES FOR UNGULATES WITHIN YELLOWSTONE NATIONAL PARK

As you tour Yellowstone in winter, you may see winterkilled animals, especially elk and bison. Usually a winterkilled carcass will be attended by a host of scavengers, including coyotes and ravens and sometimes eagles and magpies. If you are really lucky you may even see one of Yellowstone's newly introduced wolves feeding on a carcass. Their presence is an indication of the value a carcass has in the circular scheme, where the end of life for one creature means the continuation of life for many others.

Here are some other points about winterkill that may interest you. Recent research in Yellowstone has shown the following:

▲   Elk death and survival rates are more responsive to weather patterns than are those for bison, with the latter dying at a more constant rate year to year independent of weather variations;

▲   Bison also die at a more constant rate through the course of a winter, whereas elk die-offs are more concentrated in a short period of time in late winter, usually sometime in mid- to late March;

▲   On the geothermal wintering grounds both elk and bison tend to die where geothermal influence is moderate to heavy, often succumbing right next to boiling cauldrons or hissing fumaroles; females of both the dominant species of ungulates (elk and bison) tend to live longer than males; bull elk experience their peak period of die-off earlier in the winter than do cow elk;

▲   Some animals, mostly young bison, die every year by falling into hot springs, probably by being bumped in by their fellows when herds jostle close to the pools for the warmth they provide;

▲   There is convincing evidence that coyotes kill significant numbers of elk, usually young of the previous summer, by driving them into deep snow where the elk founder; coyote predation on elk seems to be especially prevalent on Yellowstone's Northern Range;

▲   The rate a winterkilled animal is consumed by scavengers varies, not surprisingly, according to the size of the carcass, from an average of one or two days for a yearling elk to an average of over thirty days for a large bull bison.

If you have the opportunity to observe Yellowstone's elk and bison for a time, you will probably see some differences in the way each species behaves and the way each uses the winter range. You might notice that elk generally have a greater affinity for forested places than do bison. Elk also are more likely to flee from people than are bison, and when they do they almost always run uphill.

Elk have a greater tendency to forage in steep places than bison. You'll often see elk on sidehills where gravity helps them remove snow from their feeding sites, which they do by scraping pits in the snow with

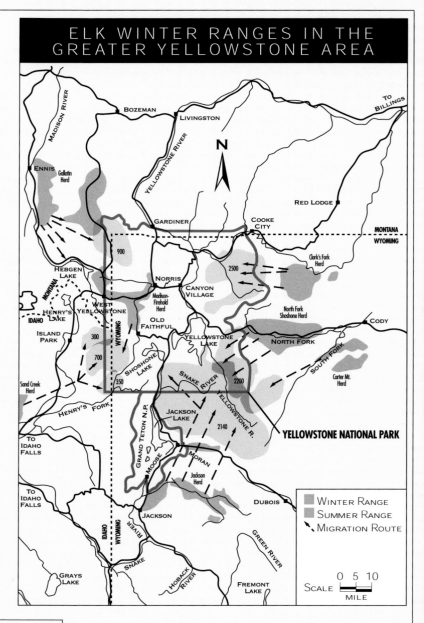

ELK WINTER RANGES IN THE GREATER YELLOWSTONE AREA

MAP COURTESY OF FRANK SINGER, YELLOWSTONE NATIONAL PARK

their forefeet. Bison, on the other hand, usually (but not always) forage by brushing the snow away with their faces, using side-to-side sweeps of their massive heads. Contrary to what some sources will tell you, bison sometimes do use their forefeet to dig through the snow; if you watch bison for very long in the winter you will see this happen.

Elk also seem to be more responsive to weather, taking refuge in trees or in the lee of topographic features in windy or very cold conditions. One research project conducted near Old Faithful found no such shelter-seeking response among bison, regardless of weather severity.

You may notice, too, that it is rare to see adult bull elk with cows of their species during winter. Bull elk have specific wintering grounds to which they are quite loyal; those places remain the same year after year and generation after generation. An example would be the area around the road crossing of Lava Creek and the Wraith Falls trailhead, about 4 or 5 miles east of Mammoth Hot Springs on the road toward Tower Junction. Another would be the area around White Creek on Grand Loop Road about 8 miles north of Old Faithful. Bull elk gather at these places every autumn, and after winter begins, it is rare to see a bull outside a bull area, though it's not uncommon to see a cow elk in a bull area.

Bison are also segregated by sex, but to a seemingly lesser degree. They also sort themselves geographically, with groups of females and young tending to inhabit larger open areas and bulls living alone or in small groups in smaller, often more out-of-the-way pockets of winter habitat. But again, this sexual segregation and geographical sorting is not nearly as pronounced as it is in elk.

Along the Madison and Firehole Rivers and possibly along the Gibbon River you may see elk feeding on aquatic vegetation. One of the plants they eat is called mare's tail, named because its length trails out in the current like a horse's tail flowing in the wind. You probably won't see bison feeding off the bottoms of rivers, though you may see members of both species standing in the rivers and feeding on riparian vegetation right at the water's edge. This aquatic feeding is made possible by the fact that the Madison, Firehole, and Gibbon Rivers never freeze because they receive so much hydrothermal inflow.

Following is a list of Yellowstone's major wildlife species and places where you have the best chance for seeing them in winter.

BISON AND BULL ELK ALONG FIRE-HOLE RIVER, MID-WAY GEYSER BASIN

MULE DEER

▲   The Northern Range, mostly around Mammoth Hot Springs and the town of Gardiner, Montana.

▲   A few (a dozen or so) around Old Faithful and nearby Biscuit Basin.

BIGHORN SHEEP

▲   The Gardner River Canyon, between Mammoth Hot Springs and Gardiner, Montana.

▲   Jackson Grade, some steep, south-facing slopes just above the confluence of Soda Butte Creek and Lamar River, about 4 miles east of Lamar Ranger Station on Northeast Entrance Road.

PRONGHORN ANTELOPE

▲   The sagebrush country around the North Entrance Station and the town of Gardiner, Montana, and along the gravel road that runs from the Gardiner High School toward Corwin Springs, Montana.

MOOSE

▲   Along Northeast Entrance Road, in the vicinity of Northeast Entrance and Silver Gate and Cooke City, Montana, specifically in the willow thickets along Soda Butte Creek.

BISON

▲   Along the Madison, Gibbon, and especially the Firehole Rivers.
▲   In Hayden Valley.
▲   In Pelican Valley (accessible only by skis or snowshoes).
▲   On the Northern Range, somewhere between upper Lamar Valley and Gardiner, Montana. The movements of this herd are more unpredictable than are those of herds elsewhere in Yellowstone.

BISON HERD AT SUNRISE, RABBIT CREEK

ELK

▲   The Northern Range (just about anywhere).
▲   The Madison, Gibbon, and Firehole River Valleys, along the rivers themselves, and in the valleys' geothermal basins.
▲   Possibly a scattered few in thermal basins elsewhere in the park.

COYOTES

▲   Just about anywhere in the park, but your best chances for seeing them are in Lamar, Hayden, and Firehole Valleys, where the open country probably harbors a generally greater density of coyotes and also makes them easier to spot.

EAGLES

▲   The Northern Range offers your best chance for seeing a golden eagle. Bald eagles are frequently seen around or near open water, especially the Madison, Gibbon, and Firehole Rivers, which never freeze, and along the Yellowstone River between Lake and Canyon, parts of which freeze only in very cold weather.
▲   Around winterkilled carcasses anywhere (both species of eagles scavenge carrion).

OTTERS

▲   On Yellowstone Lake, adjacent to the West Thumb Geyser Basin and the Potts Thermal Area just east of West Thumb Junction,

where geothermal vents on the bottom of the lake maintain openings in the ice through which the otters can fish for Yellowstone Lake cutthroat trout.

▲ Along the Yellowstone River between Lake and Canyon, especially near the Chittenden Bridge, which spans the river just upstream from the Grand Canyon of the Yellowstone.

▲ Along the Madison, Gibbon, and Firehole Rivers, again because of their ice-free nature.

WATERFOWL

▲ Along the Madison, Gibbon, and Firehole rivers and along ice-free stretches of the Yellowstone River between Lake and Canyon, especially around Fishing Bridge and around the mouths of Alum and Otter Creeks a few miles south of Canyon.

BEARS

You probably won't see any bears in the winter, but it may interest you to know that they occasionally do come out of their dens and travel around a bit. Also, some bears don't begin to hibernate until well into the winter season. In late 1986, for example, a female grizzly with a cub in Pelican Valley lucked into a windfall of carrion and stayed with it until the week of Christmas—when they were displaced from the meat by a larger bear. More commonly, bears begin to hibernate in October and November and emerge from their dens in March and April. An intensive grizzly bear research project was conducted in the thermal basins along the Firehole River from 1985 through 1990. During those years the first bear sign of the spring was located on or within one day of March 25, a date that coincided with the peak rate of die-off for that area's wintering elk and bison.

WOLVES

Wolves were reintroduced to Yellowstone in 1995 and 1996. They are most often seen on the park's Northern Range, especially in the Blacktail Plateau area and most especially in Lamar Valley. Occasional sightings are made elsewhere in the park, including the Yellowstone Lake area and the Firehole River Valley.

SUNRISE AND
ERMINE TRACKS,
FISHING BRIDGE

Geothermal Features

GROTTO GEYSER,
UPPER GEYSER
BASIN

Winter visitors to Yellowstone invariably are impressed by the inter-play between the park's hydrothermal features and cold air. Water and steam that vent through geothermal basins are heated far below the surface of the earth and emerge at virtually the same temperature, win-ter or summer. Think for a moment of the fundamental clash that occurs when water that is near the boiling point meets air that is some-times 80 or more degrees below freezing. Simple arithmetic will tell you that is a difference of nearly 275°F; simple observation will show you the dramatic results of such hydrometric strife.

Geysers explode into frigid air and send steam columns hundreds, perhaps thousands, of feet high into blue skies. Geyser rain falls back to earth, sometimes as frozen ice pellets. Hot springs and fumaroles hiss into the cold, and rime accumulates on rocks, trees, and other objects in the basins. Accumulations of rime from hydrothermal mist turn trees into white cones known in Yellowstone as ghost trees; during extended periods of cold, windless weather the amassed frost can become heavy enough to break limbs. Ice fog can persist in low-lying areas near the geyser basins until midday.

Warm water issuing from the earth creates microhabitats where communities of insects live virtually uninhibited in an otherwise wintry world. Most of these thermophilic insects are brine flies that feed on algae growing in hot springs and runoff channels. Other insects are predatory, feeding on the algae-eaters. Dead insects wash from hydrothermal runoff channels into ice-free rivers, where seasonally idle fly fishermen often notice trout rising to feed off the surface when air temperatures are well below freezing. A particularly good spot to see

trout feeding on thermophilic insects is in the Firehole River at the mouth of Ojo Caliente Spring's runoff channel. Ojo Caliente is in the Lower Geyser Basin, just downstream from the northernmost of the two bridges over the Firehole River on Fountain Flats Drive. Another interesting point about Ojo: More often than not, a young bison falls into the spring and is scalded to death sometime during the winter. And every spring, grizzly bears check Ojo's runoff channel in hopes of finding a meal of boiled buffalo meat.

Thermal basins are the margin of survival for much of Yellowstone's wildlife. Thousands of acres in the park interior are kept completely or relatively snow-free by geothermal heat rising from the earth's core. Animals are more free to move around in these reduced snow depths and actually absorb the earth's heat directly into their bodies by bedding on the warm ground. Yellowstone in winter would be a much more inhospitable place for animals such as elk and bison were it not for the area's geothermal outlets.

SAWMILL GEYSER, UPPER GEYSER BASIN

During your winter stay in Yellowstone, do try to get out and away from the lodges and snowmobiles, from the snowcoaches and crowds, from the road groomers and snowblowers, and walk or ski among the thermal basins. Look at the brine flies along runoff channels and at the frost on the trees. Maybe snap a few pictures, or stand quietly and listen to some elk or bison brush snow away from their skimpy forage; if you stand very quietly you may even be able to hear those big animals breathe, or at least catch the croak of a raven or the honk of a goose. Stop to look at and listen to the ice-free rivers flowing through a frozen landscape. Take the time to marvel at a place that is unique in all the world.

BISON IN THERMAL RUNOFF STREAM, FOUNTAIN PAINT POTS

Photography

Cold weather is the root cause of most of the mechanical challenges facing winter photographers in Yellowstone. Problems range from the inconvenient, such as having your moustache freeze to your camera back, to quite serious, such as out-and-out camera failure because of freeze-up. There are solutions to all cold-related problems, and actually the cold should not be viewed as a problem at all. It's the creator of much of Yellowstone's unique winter beauty as well as backdrops for dramatic photographs.

One way of coping with cold is to select a manual camera over battery-powered, automatic models. Batteries discharge less power in cold weather and cameras wholly dependent on them are at an inherent disadvantage. If possible, it's a good idea to keep either type of camera inside your clothing where it can absorb some of your body's warmth. Keeping your equipment inside your outer jacket (at least) will also protect it from geyser mist and spray.

Automatic cameras can be made more cold-durable by supplying them with fresh batteries before you set out. A motor drive for a single-lens reflex, 35mm camera also helps. Motor drives compensate for cold weather by providing a comparatively large power source. They are expensive accessories, though, and probably beyond the budget of most vacation photographers. Another idea is to take along two cameras and use them alternately, leaving one in the warmth of your coat while you shoot with the other. At the very least, do take along an extra set of batteries for your camera and keep them in an inner pocket.

Geyser spray is probably less of a threat to camera gear in winter than it is in the summer. That's because most winter spray is frozen by the time it returns to the earth and as ice particles simply blows by lens surfaces. Nevertheless, it is possible that liquid spray may come in contact with your equipment, from where it can evaporate and leave a

BISON IN UPPER
YELLOWSTONE
BASIN

trace of sinter (silica-based rock) in its wake. If this happens you'll have little spots of silica on your gear that will look like dust spots on a car after a spattering of raindrops. You will presumably want to avoid this situation and you can by not walking under falling geyser rain, by keeping your camera under your coat, and by using lens caps and sky-light filters. Skylight filters are a good idea in all seasons. If kept clean you can shoot through them, and if they ever are scratched or other-wise harmed (as by geyser spray) you can simply replace them for about $20 apiece, which is considerably less than the cost of replacing a lens. If you should get geyser spray on a camera lens or other optics (such as eyeglasses), don't totally despair. The consequences of such an accident aren't as dire as some sources would have you believe, because you can rub off the silica deposits. Doing so involves the risk of scratching the glass, though, and as always an ounce of prevention is worth at least a pound of cure.

Returning your camera to a warm room after a frigid outing will cause noticeable amounts of moisture to condense on the gear. The moisture won't hurt anything as long as you allow the equipment to warm thoroughly and to dry off before you take it back outside. If you should go back out before the condensation has evaporated, the moisture will freeze and you will have problems, such as fogged-over lenses that won't clear because the fog is frozen in place. Fortunately, there's no similar problem associated with taking a warm, dry camera into the cold outdoors.

A photographer needs to be well clothed for cold weather, especially if he or she plans to wait someplace for that special shot. Overdressing is preferable to underdressing; you can always remove excess clothing and carry it, but you can't put it on if you don't have it with you. Polypropylene underwear, wool pants, a sweater or an underjacket, and an outer wrap such as a Gore-Tex coat are a good formula. Good footwear, with wool socks and preferably boots with felt liners, is a must, as is a wool cap and/or a face mask. Many Yellowstone photographers wear fingerless gloves under heavier outer mitts. The fingerless undergloves provide a degree of protection when the mitts are removed for shooting. The importance of clothing cannot be overstated; a lightly clothed and cold photographer is likely to lack the patience necessary to get good shots. This is particularly true in early morning and late afternoon, when photo opportunities are often at their best but air temperatures are often at their lowest.

Photography can be combined with cross country skiing. One ski equipment manufacturer, Life Link International of Bozeman, Montana (406-586-3780), even makes a ski pole/monopod, the hilt of which can be removed to expose a threaded post that will receive the standard camera socket. Some sort of backpack is essential for carrying photo accessories while skiing (a shoulder bag is obviously out of the question). Ideally a pack used on ski trips will have a narrow profile so its sides won't interfere with your poling action. A particularly good choice for people with a lot of photo gear is the Photo Trekker pack by Lowe Pro of Chatsworth, California (818-718-6030). The Photo Trekker is padded and compartmentalized to hold lenses and accessories, and it has two outer pockets where food and water can be kept separate from photo gear. It costs about $160.

If your primary objective is photography you might choose to walk or snowshoe instead of ski. Dealing with two poles and two skis and with the inherent instability of skis can subtract a lot from your attention to photography. Walking on your own feet in shallow snow or on snowshoes in deeper snow frees your hands and gives you a more stable platform from which to work. Rental snowshoes are available at the Bear Dens at both Old Faithful Snow Lodge and Mammoth Hot Springs Hotel.

The northern tier of Yellowstone National Park usually does not have so much snow as to prohibit walking, and the geyser basins within a mile or so of Old Faithful receive so much pedestrian traffic that boardwalks are usually hardpacked and walkable. Quite often the more popular trails in the Upper Geyser Basin have two parallel paths, a set of ski tracks for skiers next to a tramped-out path for walkers. Out of consideration for skiers, please don't posthole (wallow) along their trails.

Snowmobiling with camera gear presents special challenges of its own. Basically you have to find a way to protect your equipment from the jarring of snowmobiling and still leave it accessible so you can use it to take shots along your way. A padded camera bag or pack is a good solution; on a snowmobile a shoulder-carried camera bag is feasible because it can quite readily be lashed onto your pack rack or tow sled. If you're a serious photographer and like to carry a tripod, you'll have to give it special protection while snowmobiling. The legs and mechanical connections on tripods are particularly susceptible to damage from the bouncing and jarring that are unavoidable on any snowmobile trip.

Some photographers apparently prefer specially adapted feet on their tripods for use on snow. Tripods with pointed feet for sinking into hardpacked snow and others with ski-pole tips and baskets for resting on top of soft snow have been seen in Yellowstone. The author does not see those adaptations as necessary; standard tripod feet and legs seem to do just fine.

Hydrothermal features are vastly steamier in the cold air of winter than they are in summer. Steam often obscures the geothermal vents themselves, but photographically that problem is more than compensated for by the opportunities the mist and fog create. Rising columns of steam contrast sharply with clear blue skies, and at ground level, hydrothermal steam lends itself well to creative backlighting. Just about anything can be silhouetted against a background of bright steam: skiers, bison, elk—you name it or find it. The reader may note that many of the pictures in this book are backlit shots taken in geothermal basins.

Another visual bonus of winter is the riming and crusting of trees and other objects with frost and snow. This is especially apparent on trees in close proximity to hydrothermal outlets. During cold, windless periods rime can accumulate to thicknesses of several inches on needles and branches, turning trees into almost unidentifiable white cones known in Yellowstone as ghost trees. Winter scenes and especially steamy geothermal scenes are bright. Film speeds as slow as ISO 25 can be employed without precluding hand-held shooting. As a general rule, remember to increase your exposure a stop or two more than what your light meter tells you for a snowy scene. Otherwise your scene will be underexposed, with the primary subjects, such as people, being too dark and the surrounding snow a dirty gray. This rule applies specifically to frontlit shots on snow; for backlit shots you usually should expose at just about what your light meter tells you, based on the bright background of the scene.

In addition to considering the location of the sun, photographers in geyser basins have to take note of wind direction. You may set up for a certain shot according to where the sun will be relative to your subject only to have the subject partially or totally obscured by windblown clouds of steam. Prevailing winds in Yellowstone originate from the southwest. Perhaps just as important to the photographer are local thermal currents. Generally those currents are down-drainage, cold-air currents at night and up-drainage, warm-air (relatively speaking) currents during the day. This is an important point because air movements often reverse around sunrise and sunset, just when photographers are most likely to be working. This flow reversal is especially significant around Old Faithful Geyser, which is situated at the upper end of the Upper Geyser Basin. The area around Old Faithful usually drains free of steam through the night. Shortly after dawn, just when photographers are looking for a sunrise shot of the famous geyser, the cold-air drainage around Old Faithful reverses and accumulated steam from the scores of thermal features downstream drifts up to and around Old Faithful, often veiling it from sight.

CASTLE GEYSER, UPPER GEYSER BASIN

A few other tips about photographing geysers: If possible, try to get your picture just after the geyser erupts when you can capture the entire water and steam column in your frame. This is tough to do and it won't work out for you every time because steam forms and rises quickly when boiling water comes in contact with frigid air. In addition to framing the eruption, try to snap your picture when it's possible to distinguish water from steam within the column. Finally, meter the eruptive column and set your exposure accordingly. If you manage to do all these things at once, you should come away with a strong image.

The best places for finding wildlife accustomed to people and therefore easier to photograph are the Mammoth Hot Springs area and the Madison, Gibbon, and Firehole River Valleys, with the last including the Old Faithful area. You will find primarily elk and mule deer around Mammoth and bison and elk along the three river valleys. You can also find large numbers of bison in Hayden Valley and along the east side of Yellowstone Lake. The classic shots of wildlife and thermal features can most readily be put together in the geyser basins along the Firehole Valley. Please be considerate of the wildlife at all times, even forgoing a photograph if taking it means disturbing the animals. Remember, when you're back in the warmth of your room at night, cleaning your camera gear and drinking hot chocolate, those animals will still be outside, working on the problem of survival.

FOLLOWING PAGE:
SNOWSHOE HARE
TRACKS AT
SUNSET,
NORTHERN
YELLOWSTONE

"Gut-wrenching plotlines, and infinite heart."
—DANEET STEFFENS, *BOSTON GLOBE*

"[It has] a sardonic, streetwise voice—like a pissed off
conscience, telling a cautionary tale."
—ANTHONY BREZNICAN, *ENTERTAINMENT WEEKLY*

"One of the great New York City novels ever written."
—MIKE LUPICA, *DAILY NEWS* (NEW YORK)

"Shattering. . . . Boisterous [and] profane."
—JANET MASLIN, *NEW YORK TIMES*

"A brilliant novel, rich in language, conflict, setting, and character."
—MARK RUBINSTEIN, *HUFFINGTON POST*

"A scorcher."
—MARILYN STASIO, *NEW YORK TIMES BOOK REVIEW*

"Ready-made for Hollywood. . . . A big, fat book of fast-moving fiction."
—NEELY TUCKER, *WASHINGTON POST*

"Heartbreakingly beautiful and unforgiving."
—ROBERT ANGLEN, *ARIZONA REPUBLIC*

"Riveting, infuriating, and ultimately deeply moving."
—BILGE EBIRI, *VILLAGE VOICE*

"I stopped everything I was doing to read it straight through."
—GREG ILES

"[An] epic novel of devastating moral complexity."
—PUBLISHERS WEEKLY (STARRED REVIEW)